I0816394

USBORNE

UNDERSTANDING AI

Designed by Jamie Ball and Tom Lalonde

AI expert:
Professor Michael Wooldridge,
University of Oxford

Contents

Usborne Quicklinks

For links to websites where you can see how AI is used in everyday life, try games made with machine learning, and explore topics from this book with videos and activities, go to **usborne.com/Quicklinks** and type in the title of this book.

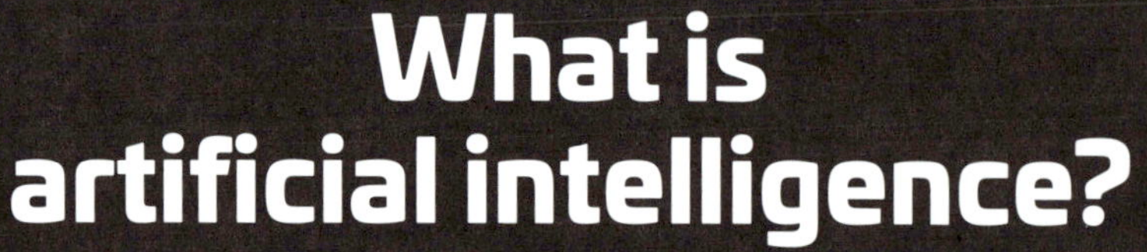

What is artificial intelligence?

Artificial intelligence (**AI**, for short) is the ability of a machine to act or behave as a human can.

OK, so I'm going to do a survey to see what my friends think AI is.

Social media guessing what you want to see!

I think it's things like chatbots, only more clever. You can talk to them as if they were a real person.

Hi, how can I help you today?

Can you recommend a park in my area?

Sure, Edith Park has cafés, tennis courts and a pool.

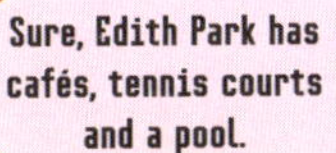

Robots that are going to take everyone's jobs away.

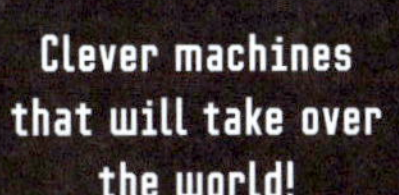

Clever machines that will take over the world!

ADVANCED QUANTUM MECHANICS

The ability of a computer to think and learn.

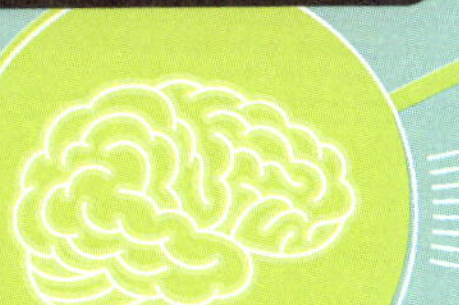

Machines that are really, really smart.

It means machines that can think and are aware of things just like humans.

OK, interesting survey. But are these things true? Some of them sound scary!

I don't know. What we really need to do is ask an expert!

I work on AI. I can try to answer your questions.

Turn the page to find out more.

So what ACTUALLY *is* AI?

Well, different experts might answer that question differently. But most agree that you can make sense of what AI *is*...
...by looking at some of the things AI can *do*.

Let's start by looking at an ordinary machine that doesn't have any AI in it.

Vacuum cleaner

Whirrrrrrr

A person pushes a vacuum cleaner where they want it to go. It's up to THEM to avoid bumping into things.

The machine will suck up anything it can, including socks, pet toys, coins, your homework...

Its suction strength remains the same, whatever the surface.

OK, so there's definitely no AI in there.

Yup! Just a basic machine that the human has to control in every way.

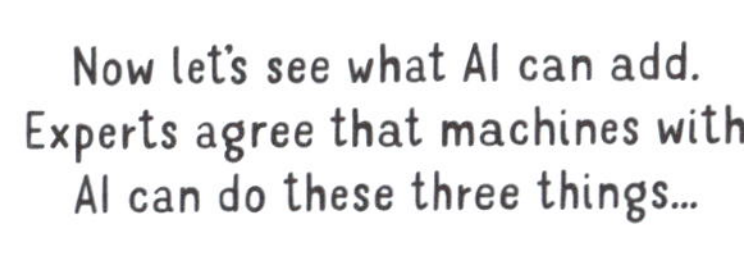

Autonomous AI vacuum cleaner (Robovac)

Autonomous means it doesn't need to be pushed or guided by a human.

1. They can use **data** to identify things in the world around them.

So Robovac has SENSORS, and its AI uses the data it senses to learn where obstacles are – and avoid them.

2. They can assess data, and use it to make *predictions, recommendations* or *decisions.*

Robovac can decide on the best suction strength, depending on whether the surface is carpet or hard floor.

3. They can *learn* and *adapt*. Once you've trained AI programs to do something, they can improve their ability to do that thing without anyone having to do anything else.

Robovac can learn to recognize and avoid sucking up things you don't want it to.

Can Robovac answer questions too, like you can, Fizzy?

No, it can't. Currently, each AI device is only good at one thing.

Computer scientists are trying to develop something called **Artificial General Intelligence (AGI),** which would be able to learn to do any mental task.

How far has AI come?

Artificial intelligence can make a vacuum cleaner whiz around a room without a human needing to lift a finger. What else can it do? And what *could* it do tomorrow?

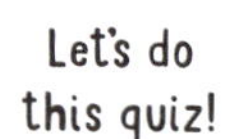

CAN AI...

1. ...beat a human at chess? A  B  C 

2. ...spot subtle signs of a disease on a scan of a patient? A  B  C 

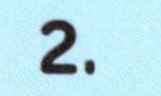

3. ...make and grow a human baby? A   B  C 

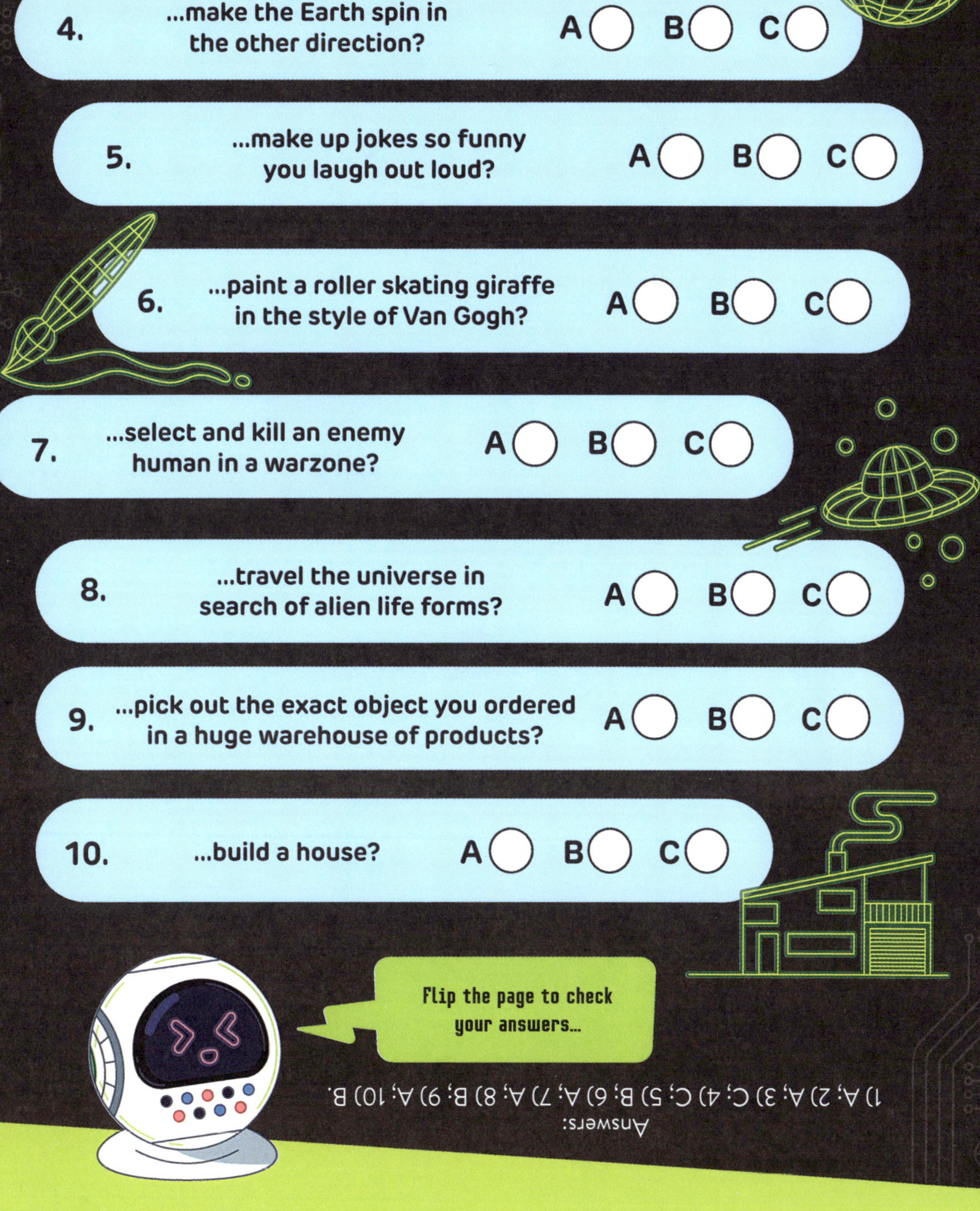

Although AI can already do a lot of things, many AI programs make mistakes. As well as developing new AI tools, researchers are trying to make sure existing AI systems are reliable and trustworthy.

How will the world change?

Lots of people think that AI will transform the world. But nobody knows yet how extreme the changes will be, or whether they will be mostly GOOD or mostly BAD. This diagram shows a range of potential scenarios.

POSITIVE IMPACT

Daily life gets easier as technology improves.

What should I eat?

Your fridge contains all the ingredients for jerk chicken.

People can choose how to spend their time, because robots do all the work. Everyone gets a basic income to live on.

I'm sunbathing.

I'm learning about the history of art.

SMALL CHANGE

It gets harder to keep your personal data private.

Robots replace real people in their jobs, leaving lots of people without enough money to live on.

NEGATIVE IMPACT

Left to right, the changes get bigger, are less likely and will take longer to happen. Up to down, the changes go from good to bad.
AI is used to cure all diseases and slow down ageing.
I'm 120 and I feel GREAT!
People use AI to solve the world's problems, such as climate change and global inequality.
BIG
CHANGE
Robots become smarter than humans and kill off all of humanity.
AI is used to *create* new diseases, used as weapons in wars.
I guess our future depends on how clever AI technology becomes.
It's not just that. How people design, use, control and respond to AI will decide our future too.

I wonder what's going on inside my circuits?

Chapter 1
How does AI work?

All computers complete tasks by following instructions called **algorithms**. But when a computer uses artificial intelligence, these algorithms are so complex they can tell the computer to *teach itself* new skills.

How do computing experts get computers to be that smart? Well, they find inspiration from the human brain.

No one knows exactly how human brains work. But we do know that they contain billions of brain cells, called **neurons**, which connect with each other in complex ways. When we think, learn and solve problems, information flows between neurons.

Inspired by neurons, AI is often programmed with a type of coding known as an **artificial neural network**. This instructs a computer to manage information similarly to the way experts think a human brain does.

Hard and soft

A computer is made up of lots of different parts, which can be divided into two main categories: **hardware** and **software**.

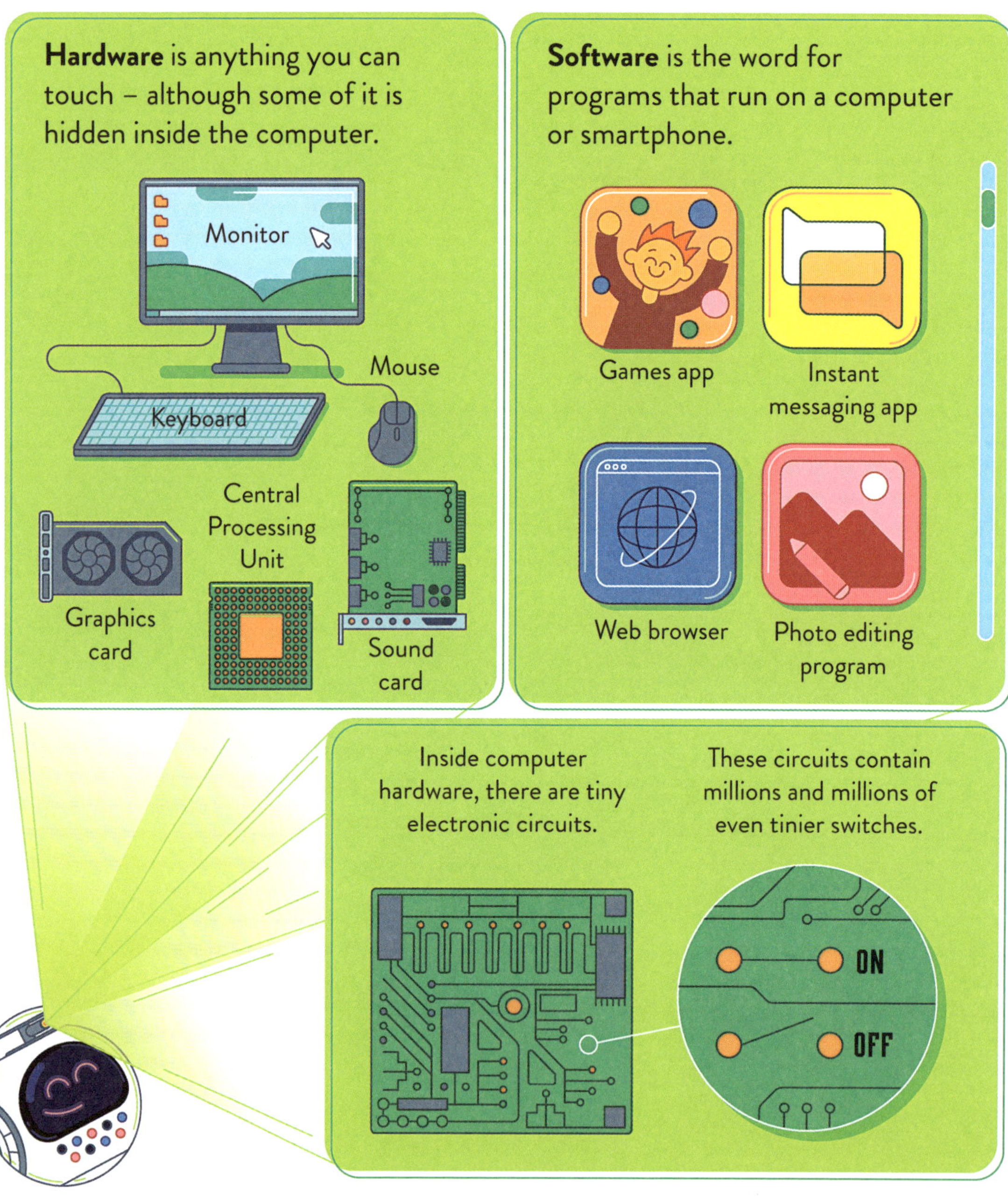

A switch can either be ON or OFF. Software tells the computer which switches to turn on, and when to turn them off. This sets the exact path that electricity takes through the circuit, enabling the computer to process information.

Follow the steps

Software is made up of **algorithms**. These are precise sets of step-by-step instructions which the computer follows to complete a task. When a computer follows an algorithm, it's like a human following a recipe.

Hey Fizzy, how should I cook this pasta?

Here are some instructions...

The steps in an algorithm follow a logical order.

The instructions are specific, so they produce the same result each time.

Weigh out 75g (2.6oz) of pasta per person.

Bring a pot of water to the boil.

Add a tablespoon of salt to the water.

Add the pasta to the pot.

Simmer for 9 minutes.

Taste one piece of pasta.

Is it cooked yet?

Algorithms can contain questions, which lead to a choice between two actions.

NO: Simmer for one more minute.

YES: Drain pasta, add sauce and serve.

Algorithms can have loops, where a sequence is repeated until a certain condition has been met.

When a computer runs an algorithm, each of the steps causes an electronic change, as the tiny switches turn on or off. Some algorithms use AI. But the example above doesn't, as the computer is told exactly what to do and doesn't need to work anything out for itself.

Inputs and outputs

One simple way to think about how computers work is that you put something in at one end, and something else comes out of the other end. The thing that goes in is called an **input**, and what comes out is called an **output**.

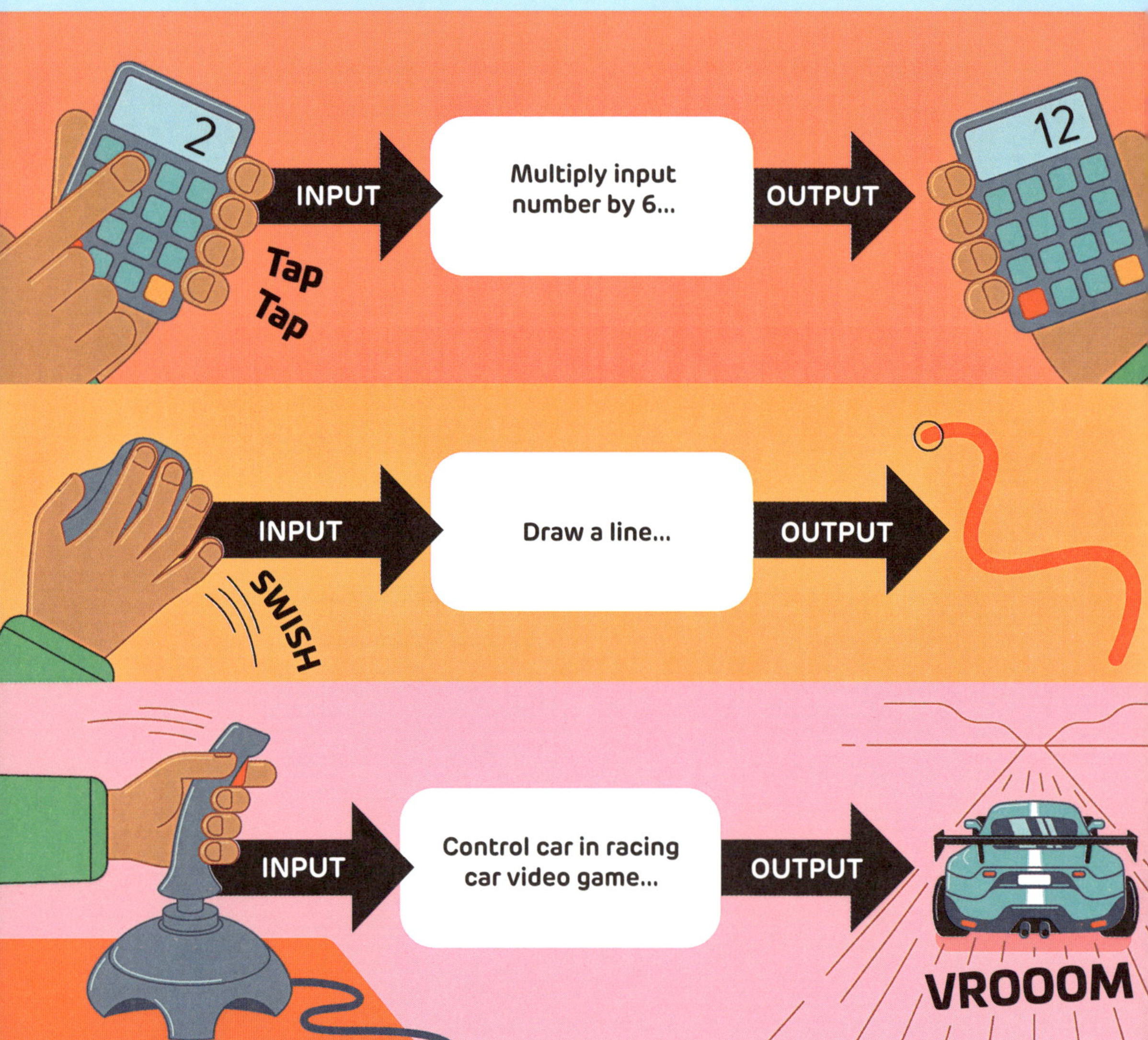

The three examples above are relatively straightforward. They don't require AI, because the input – combined with a simple algorithm – tells the computer exactly what it needs to do.

But in the more complicated examples below, a computer needs to use AI to learn how to turn the input into the output. Over time it will gradually get better and better at it.

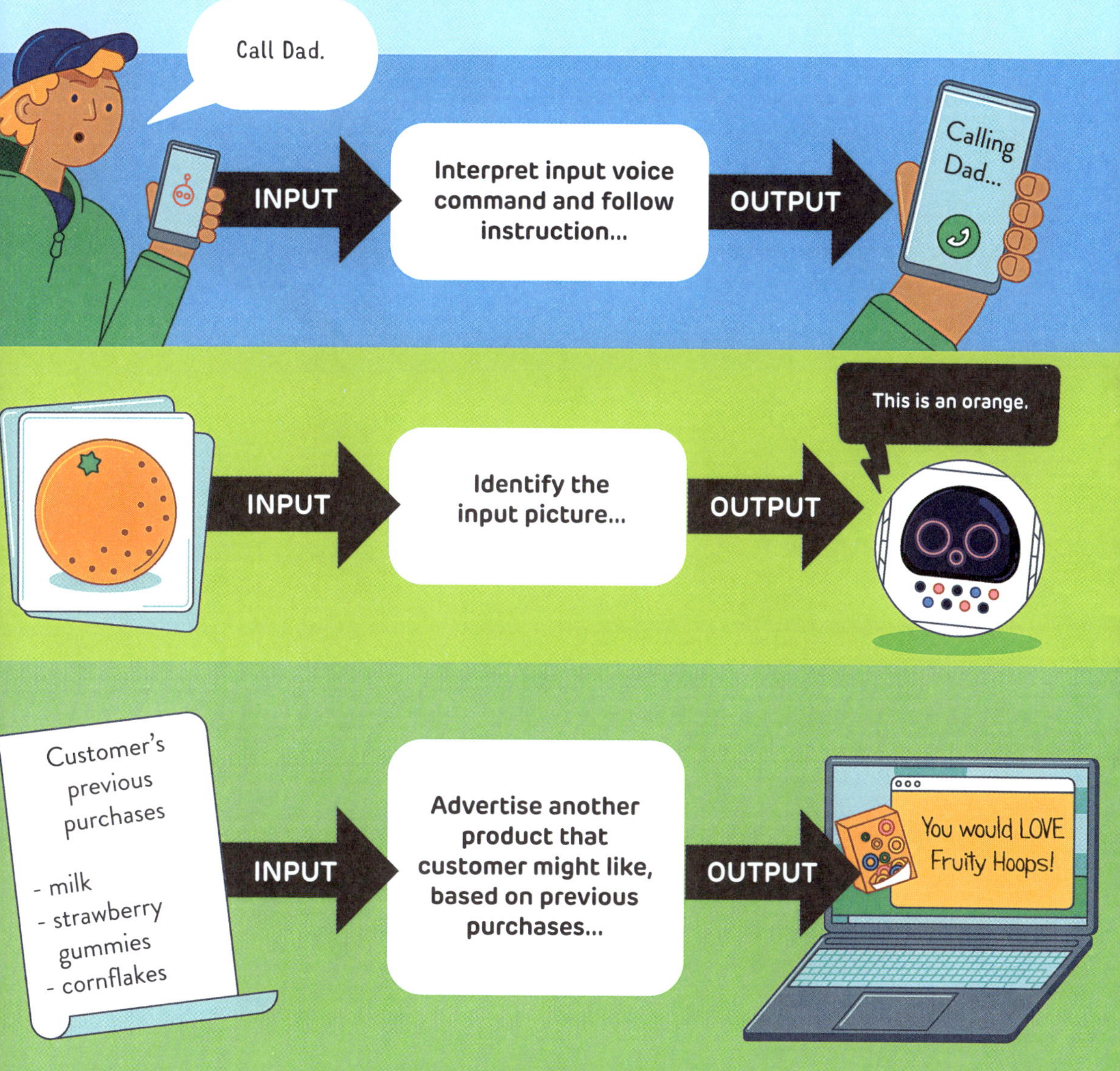

AI is getting smarter all the time. It is becoming capable of more and more complex processes to turn inputs into outputs. Turn the page to find out more.

AI or not AI?

In 1997, a supercomputer called Deep Blue beat the world chess champion, Garry Kasparov. This was a milestone in intelligent computing – the first time a computer had ever beaten a reigning chess champion.

Deep Blue was programmed with algorithms to study 200 million potential chess moves in a second, and choose the one most likely to lead to victory.

A human moved the actual pieces, following instructions from Deep Blue.

After playing six games, Deep Blue was the overall winner.

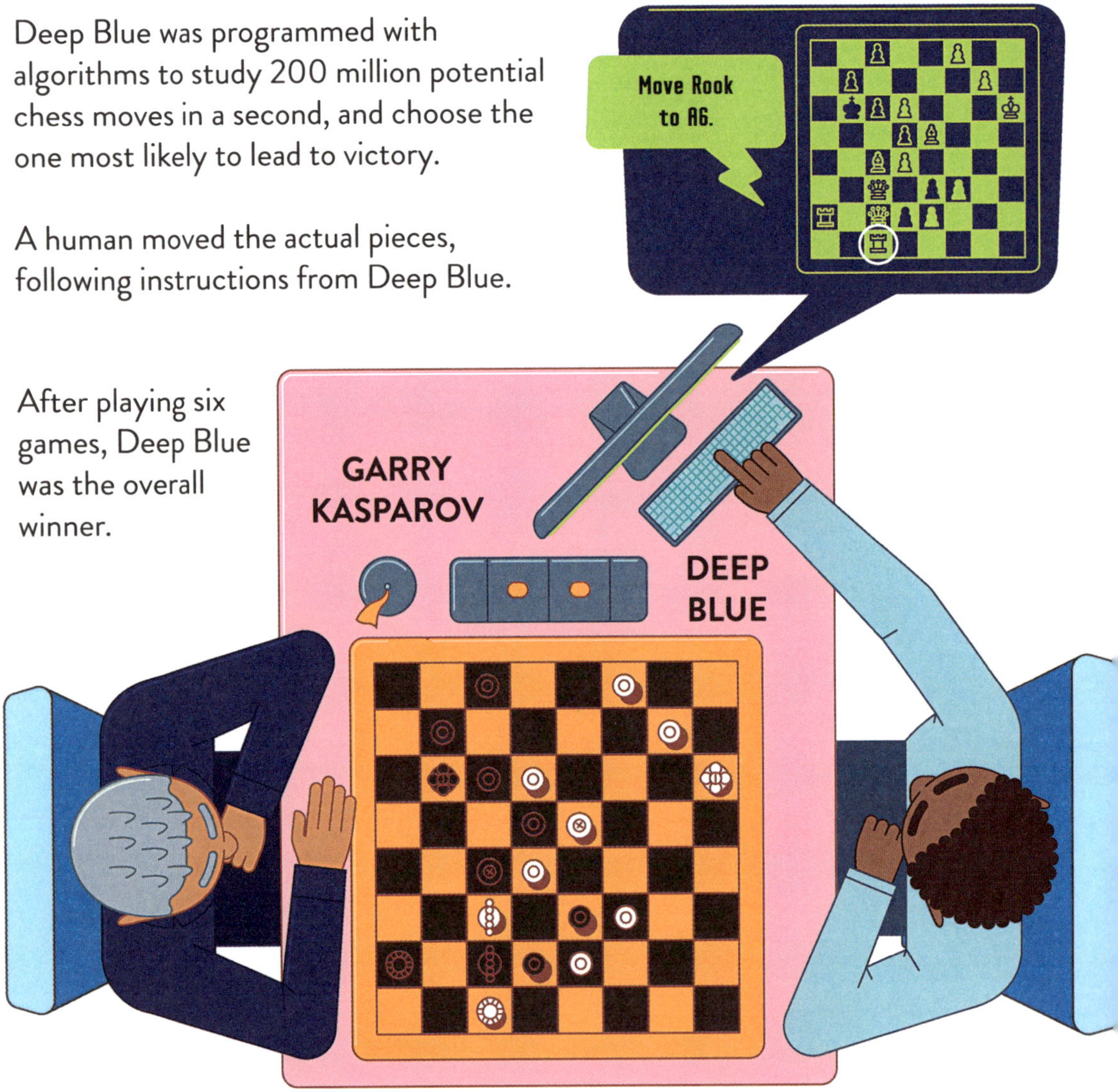

Deep Blue's hugely complex algorithms were written by a mix of top coders and chess experts, who worked together to build it.

At the time, it was considered to be a milestone in artificial intelligence. But by today's standards, Deep Blue isn't considered to have used AI. That's because it was simply following instructions.

Self-teaching machines

Today, coders don't need to lay out precise instructions for what a machine should do in *every* potential situation. Instead, they can write algorithms telling machines to teach themselves.

AlphaGo

In 2016, a computer program called AlphaGo beat a human at the strategy board game, Go. The human was Lee Sedol, a professional who is considered one of the best in the history of the game.

Unlike Deep Blue, AlphaGo didn't have a database of moves to consider. It had *taught itself* to play Go, first by watching recorded games, and then by playing against itself. So, it *did* use artificial intelligence.

Learning with labels

When a computer learns how to do something, it's called **machine learning**. There are different types of machine learning, but each one involves a **training phase**, a **predictions phase** and a **test phase**.

Here's how one type of machine learning works.

Training computers often requires many, many hours of human work at the start. (Companies that promote their own AI software rarely talk about this.)

A computer can process thousands of images quickly, but it needs a lot of computing power to do that.

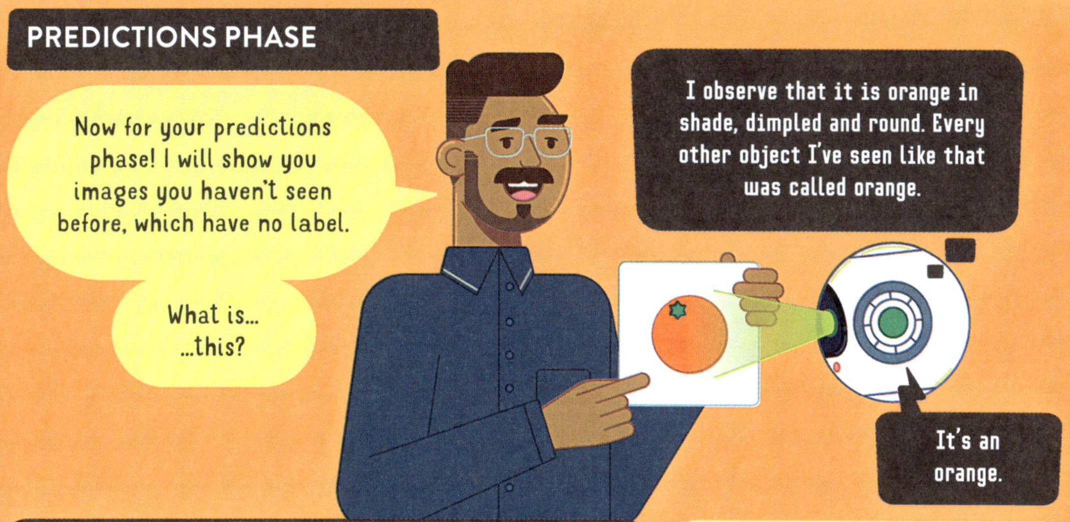

PREDICTIONS PHASE

Now for your predictions phase! I will show you images you haven't seen before, which have no label.

What is... ...this?

I observe that it is orange in shade, dimpled and round. Every other object I've seen like that was called orange.

It's an orange.

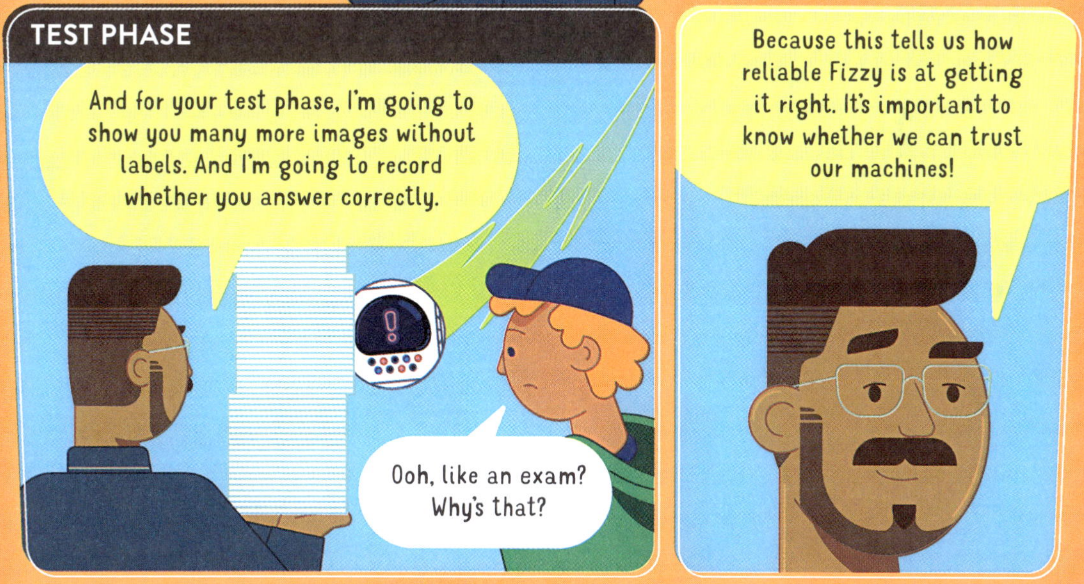

TEST PHASE

And for your test phase, I'm going to show you many more images without labels. And I'm going to record whether you answer correctly.

Ooh, like an exam? Why's that?

Because this tells us how reliable Fizzy is at getting it right. It's important to know whether we can trust our machines!

This type of machine learning is called **supervised learning** because the machine can't do it without a human putting labels on the training data.

Spotting patterns

In another type of machine learning, a computer is given data with no labels. It's then left on its own to find patterns within data, and group together similar items, without being told exactly what to look for.

This method, called **unsupervised learning**, is useful because humans don't have to spend time naming all the data. Also, a computer can often spot patterns in data that are too subtle for a human to notice.

Unsupervised learning can be used to identify unusual patterns in data, which is useful for:

Detecting credit card fraud...

Preventing computers from getting hacked...

Spotting early signs that a machine needs maintenance, before it actually breaks down...

Reward / Punish

Have you ever played a car racing game where you're racing against a computer? Did you wonder how the computer got so good? It was probably trained using a machine learning system known as **reinforcement learning**.

In reinforcement learning, a computer learns by being given "rewards" when it does something right, and "punishments" when it does something wrong.

The computer doesn't have strict instructions about exactly how to drive its car. At first, it bumps and crashes often.

The computer chooses its exact moves randomly. Sometimes, just by chance, it does something very clever.

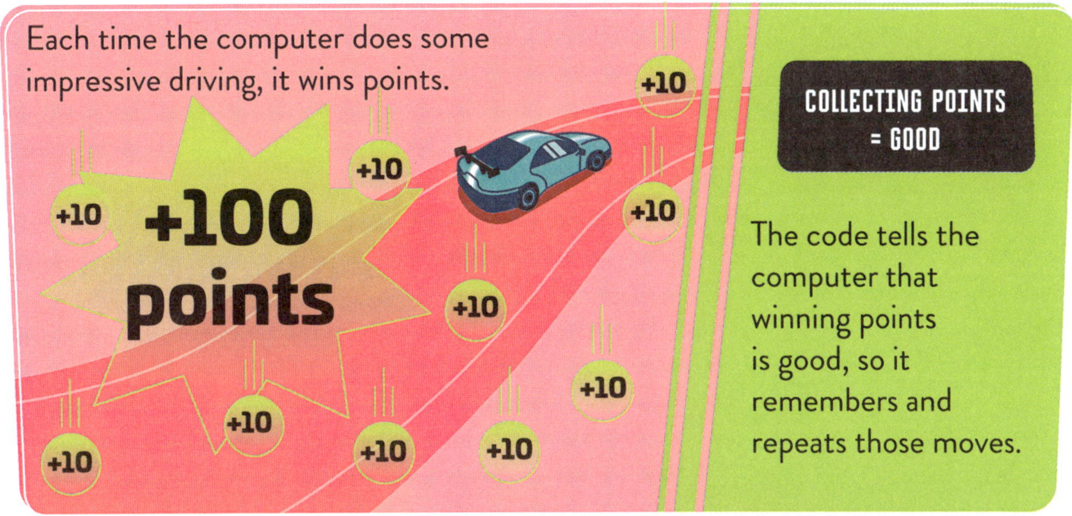

During the training phase, the car drives thousands of times around the course. It never gets tired and steadily improves. It teaches itself skills along the way, which help it once it's playing against a human.

Numbers, numbers, numbers...

Before a computer can deal with an input – ANY input – it must be converted to numbers. All inputs can be converted to numbers, whether they are images, text or sounds.

For example, here's how an image of an orange is converted into numbers:

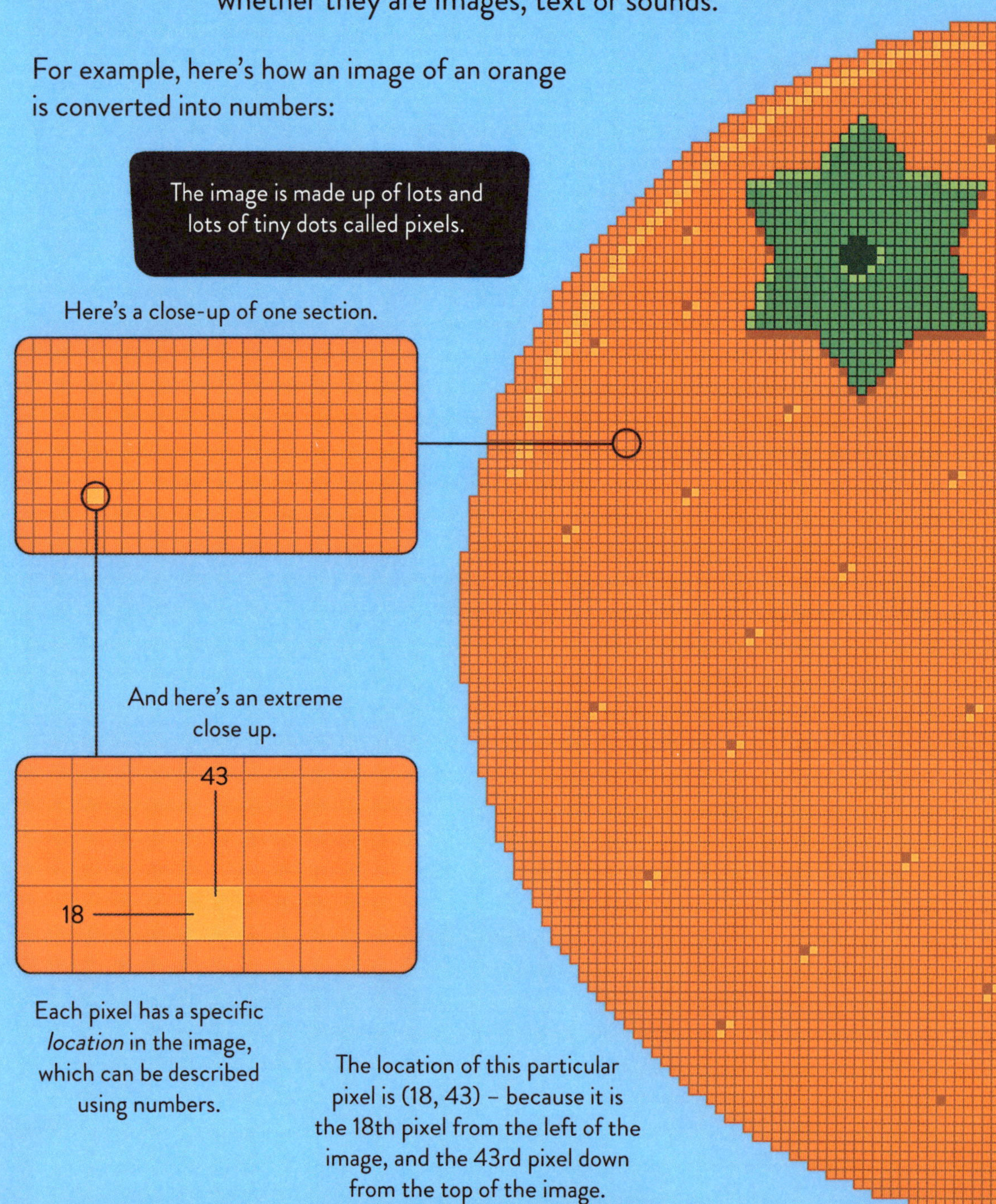

Each pixel has a specific *location* in the image, which can be described using numbers.

The location of this particular pixel is (18, 43) – because it is the 18th pixel from the left of the image, and the 43rd pixel down from the top of the image.

15°C / 59°F Mostly cloudy

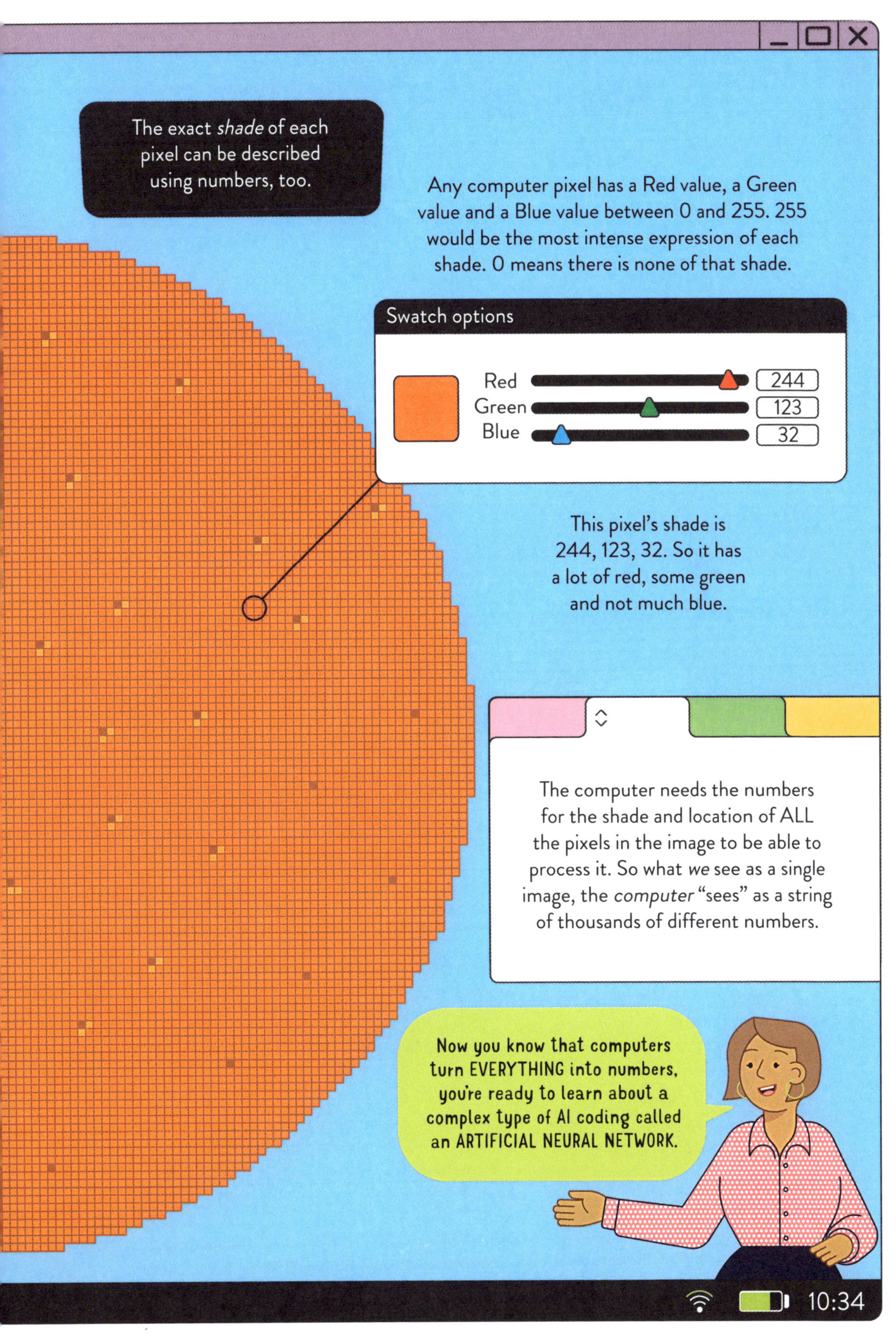
The exact *shade* of each pixel can be described using numbers, too.
Any computer pixel has a Red value, a Green value and a Blue value between 0 and 255. 255 would be the most intense expression of each shade. 0 means there is none of that shade.
Swatch options
Red
Green
Blue
244
123
32
This pixel's shade is 244, 123, 32. So it has a lot of red, some green and not much blue.
The computer needs the numbers for the shade and location of ALL the pixels in the image to be able to process it. So what *we* see as a single image, the *computer* "sees" as a string of thousands of different numbers.
Now you know that computers turn EVERYTHING into numbers, you're ready to learn about a complex type of AI coding called an ARTIFICIAL NEURAL NETWORK.
10:34

Neural networks

One common way to get a computer to learn is to create something called an **artificial neural network (ANN)**. This is a way of telling it how to process information, inspired by how human neurons communicate with each other.

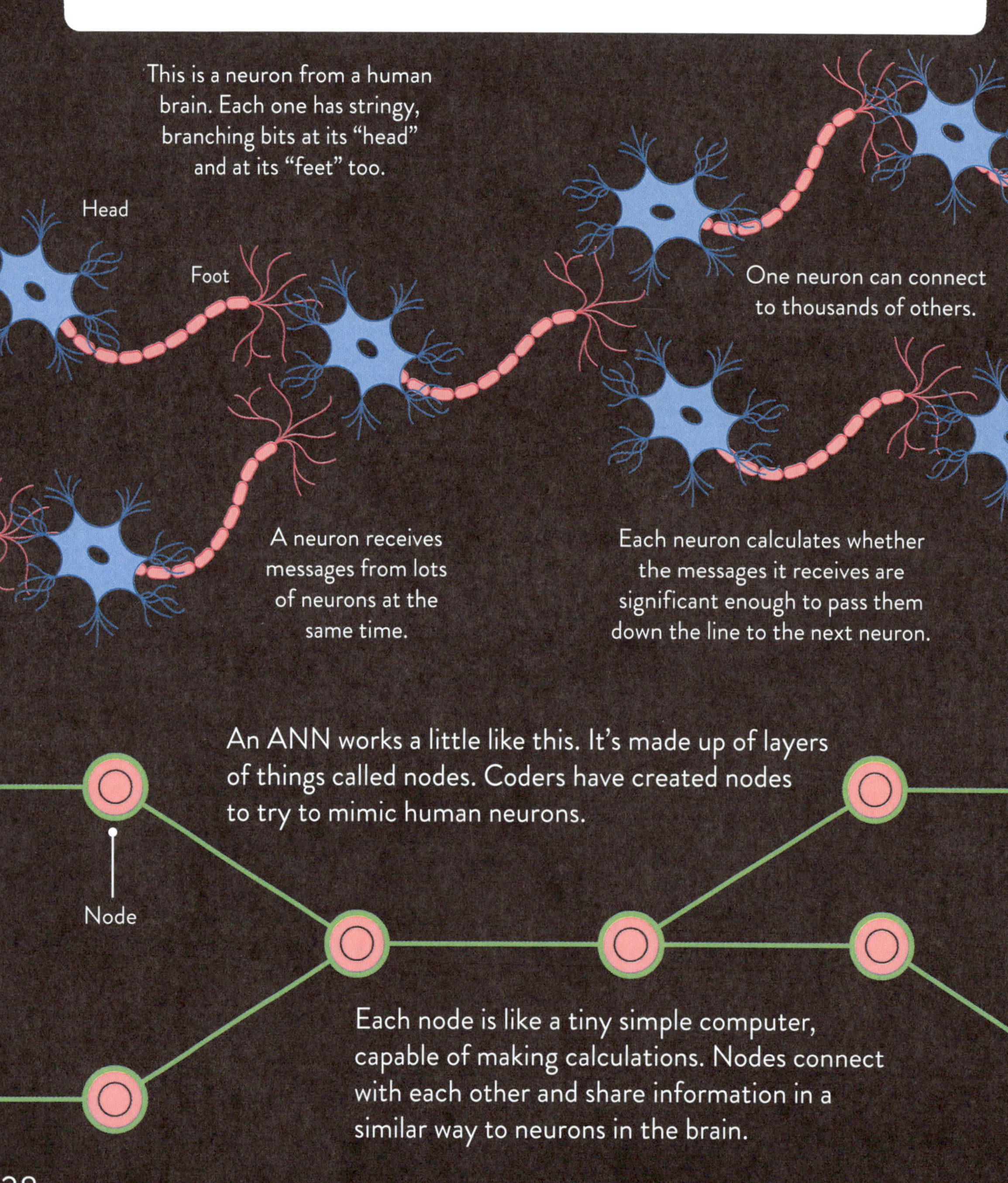

AI devices, such as Fizzy, are coded with ANNs. When Fizzy is learning to identify an orange, the *input* is fed into the network and is processed in several layers before it emerges from the network as the *output*.

The numbers describing the orange are fed into the input nodes.

The data is passed on to nodes in the inner layer. At each connection, the numbers are multiplied by another number, which is described as the **weight** of that connection.

The data is multiplied by a weight again, as it is passed to nodes in the output layer.

A new number is spat out of the output layer of the network. The computer interprets this output number as a word: ORANGE.

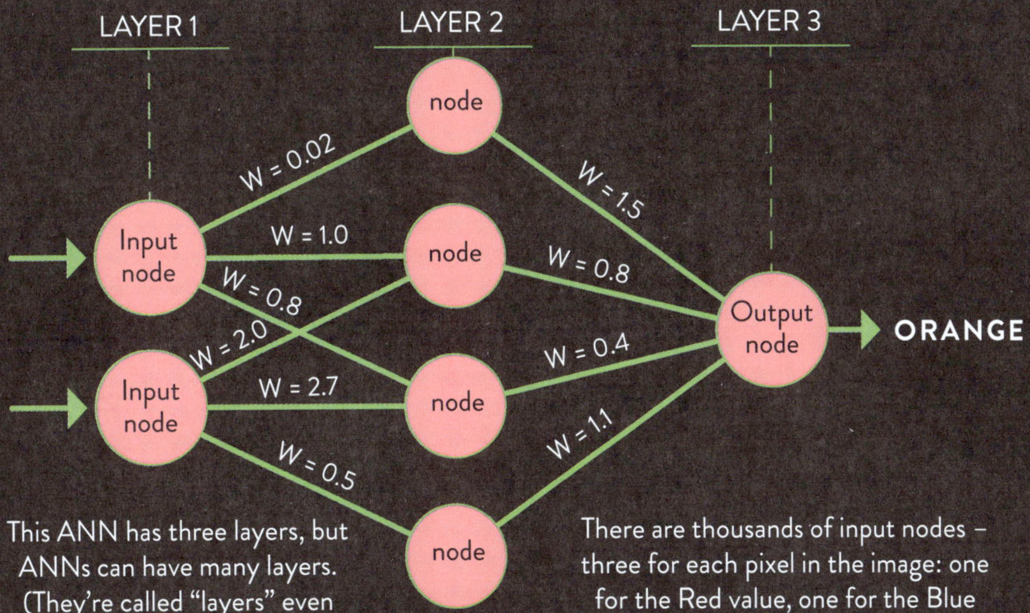

LAYER 1

LAYER 2

LAYER 3

Input node

Input node

node

node

node

node

Output node

ORANGE

W = 0.02

W = 1.0

W = 0.8

W = 2.0

W = 2.7

W = 0.5

W = 1.5

W = 0.8

W = 0.4

W = 1.1

This ANN has three layers, but ANNs can have many layers. (They're called "layers" even though they're often depicted as columns.)

There are thousands of input nodes – three for each pixel in the image: one for the Red value, one for the Blue value and one for the Green.

Wait! Is an ANN a physical bit of hardware? Like a bunch of blobs wired together?

No. An ANN is a series of steps written in computer code.

OK. I'm confused about how "weights" work.

Don't worry, I'll explain more on the next page.

Learning through mistakes

At first, an ANN trained by supervised learning works out how to do something by producing a random, *wrong* output. By comparing its wrong output to the correct output, it figures out how to get it right next time.

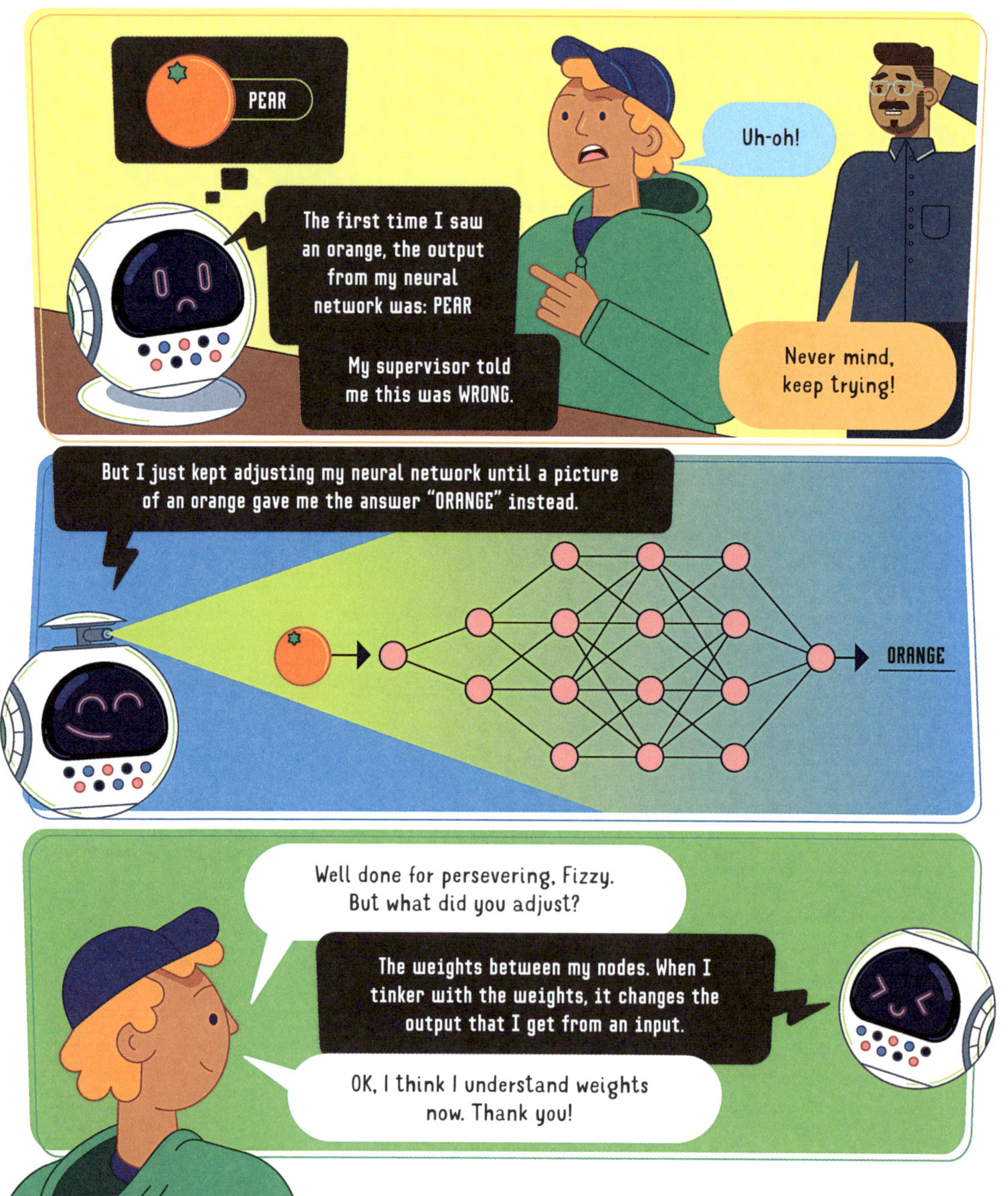

When a computer learns to identify an image, it's like a big numbers game between the human and the computer. The picture AND the weights in between the nodes AND the output word are all represented by numbers. Here's a simplified version of how it goes...

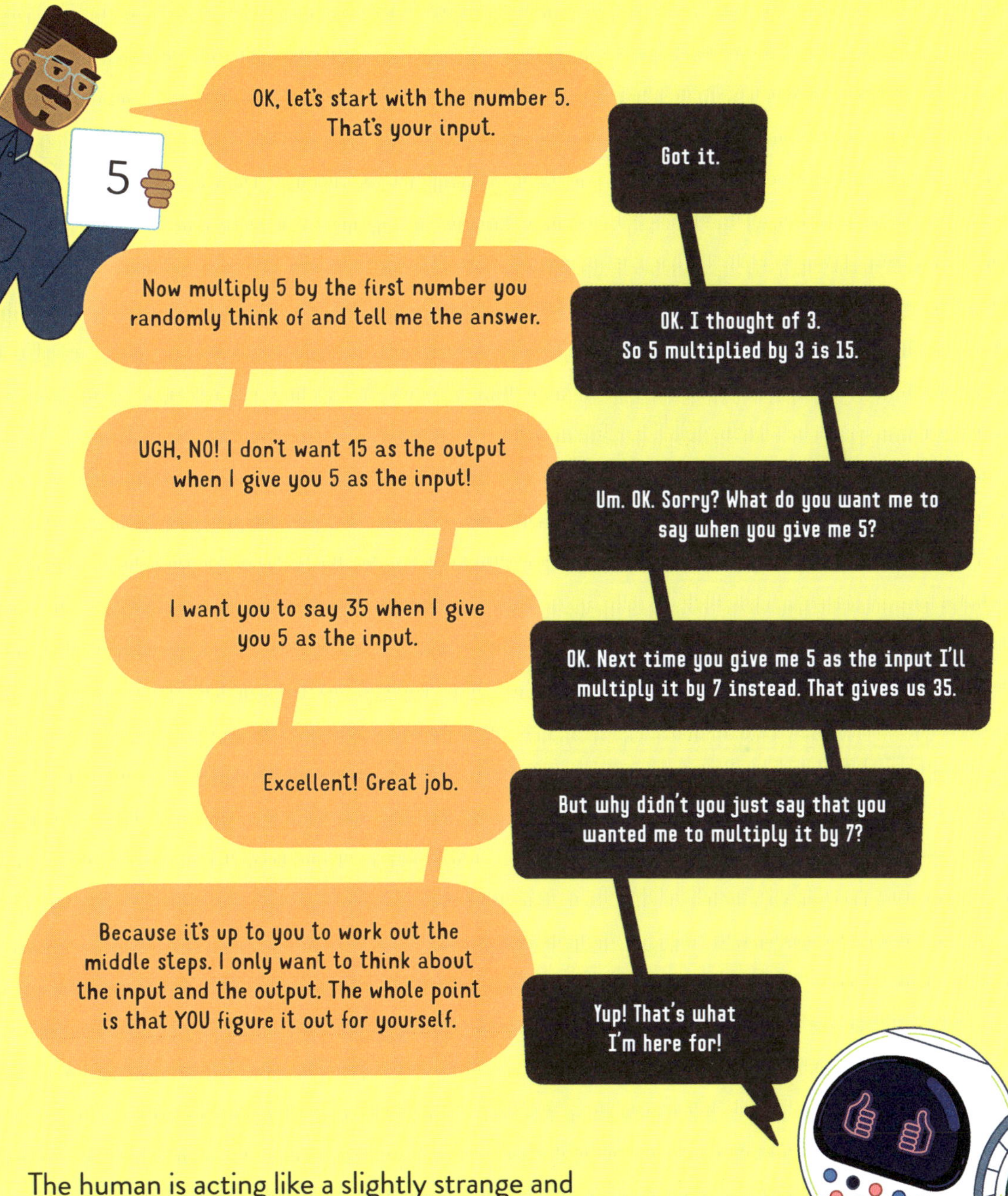

The human is acting like a slightly strange and infuriating teacher. But the computer doesn't mind. It will search for the right middle step until it comes up with the correct output.

Deep learning

Artificial neural networks with *many* inner layers are called **deep neural networks.** Machine learning using these is known as **deep learning.**

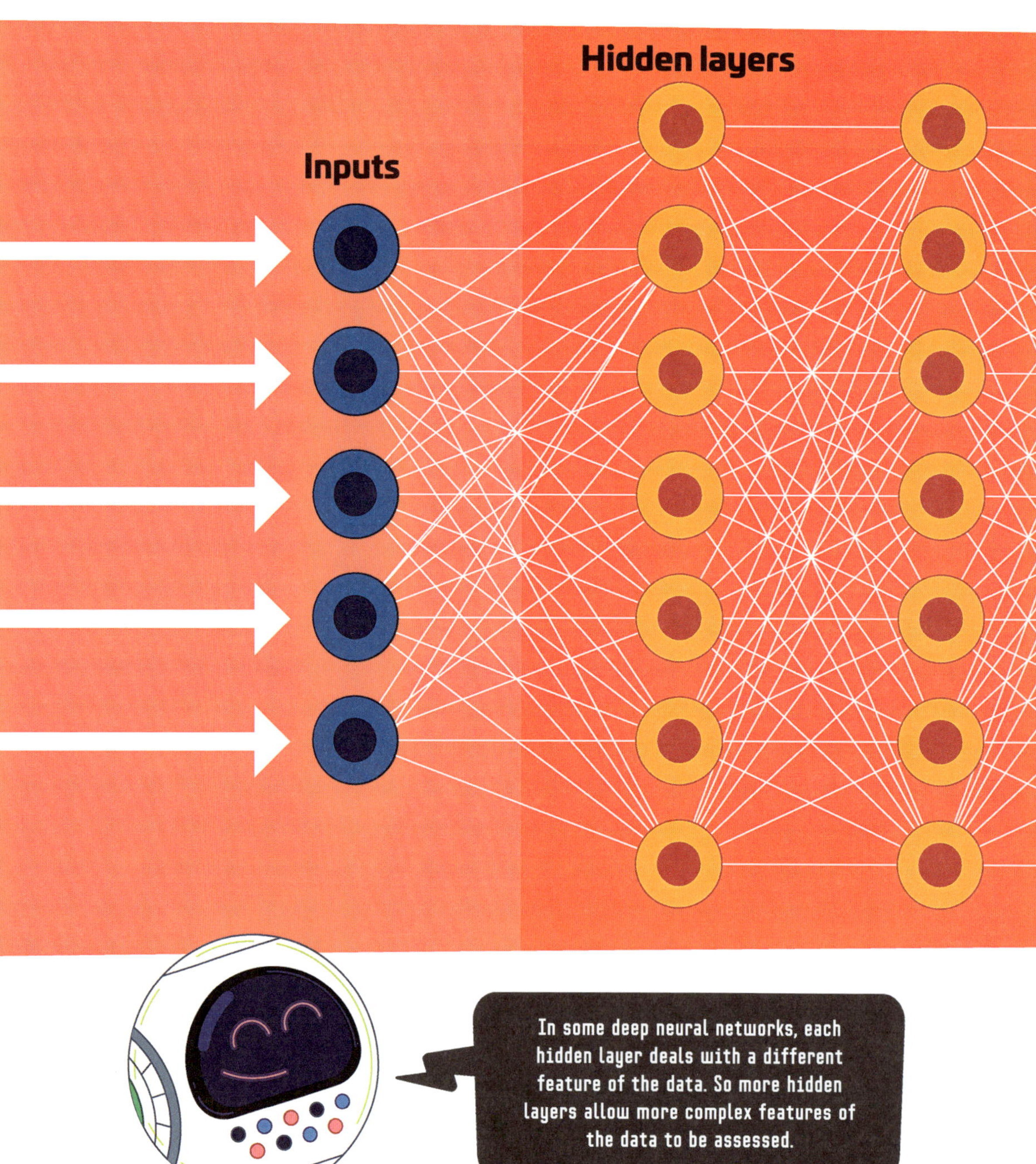

In some deep neural networks, each hidden layer deals with a different feature of the data. So more hidden layers allow more complex features of the data to be assessed.

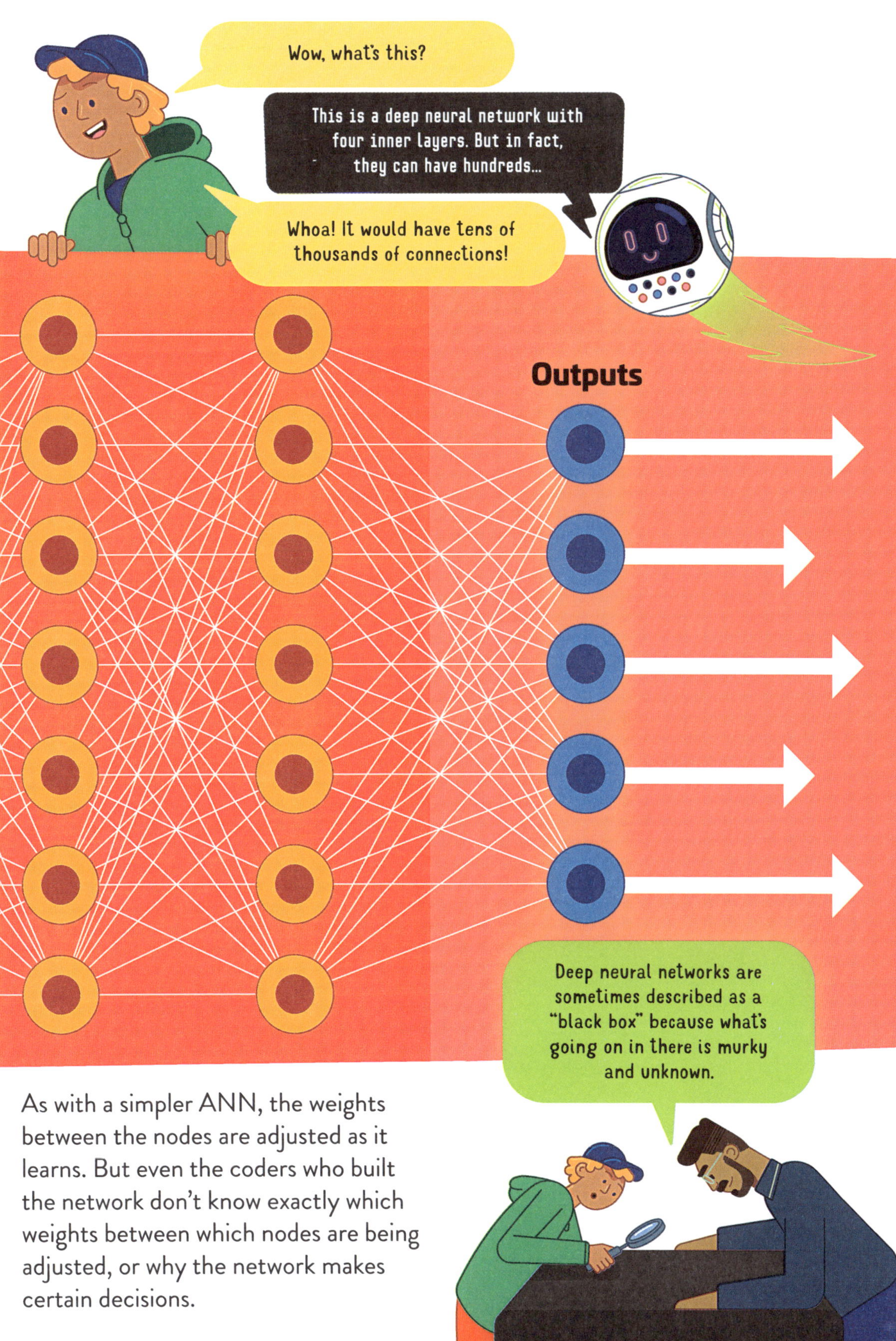

As with a simpler ANN, the weights between the nodes are adjusted as it learns. But even the coders who built the network don't know exactly which weights between which nodes are being adjusted, or why the network makes certain decisions.

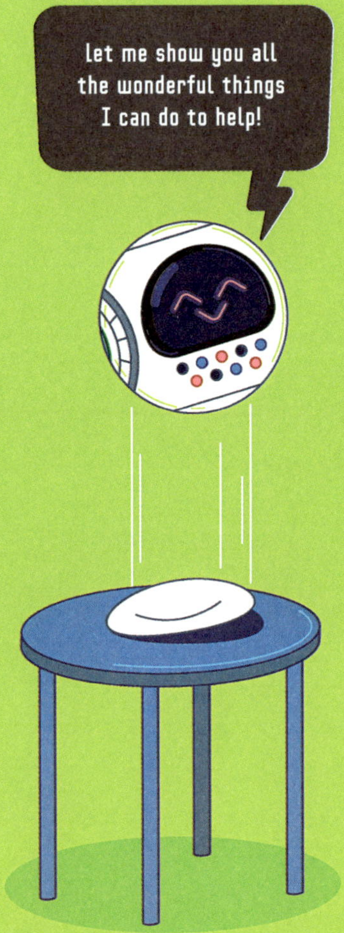

let me show you all
the wonderful things
I can do to help!

Chapter 2
AI in action

The idea of AI was first dreamed up by mathematics and computing professors in the 1950s. They wanted to find out if a machine could be intelligent in the same way as a human.

Here, in the 21st century, AI is being used in practical ways, to help with things such as making decisions, predictions and recommendations. Turn the page to see a whole range of examples.

But beware! There are limits to what AI can do, and how much it will be able to help without causing problems.

Where AI can help

Most people encounter AI through smartphones or computers, but AI programs have been built into many other machines, including robots. Here are some examples of how AI tools are being used today.

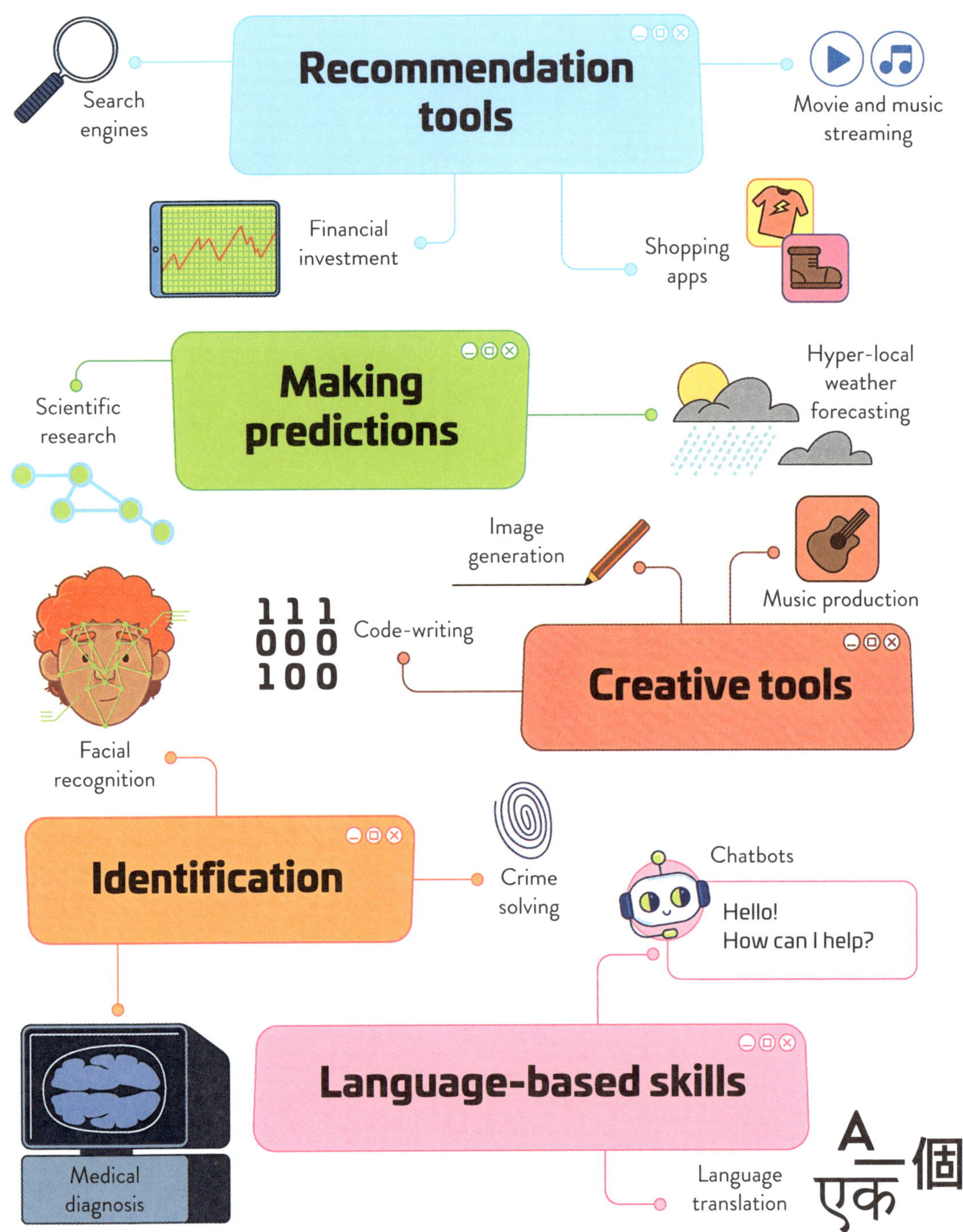

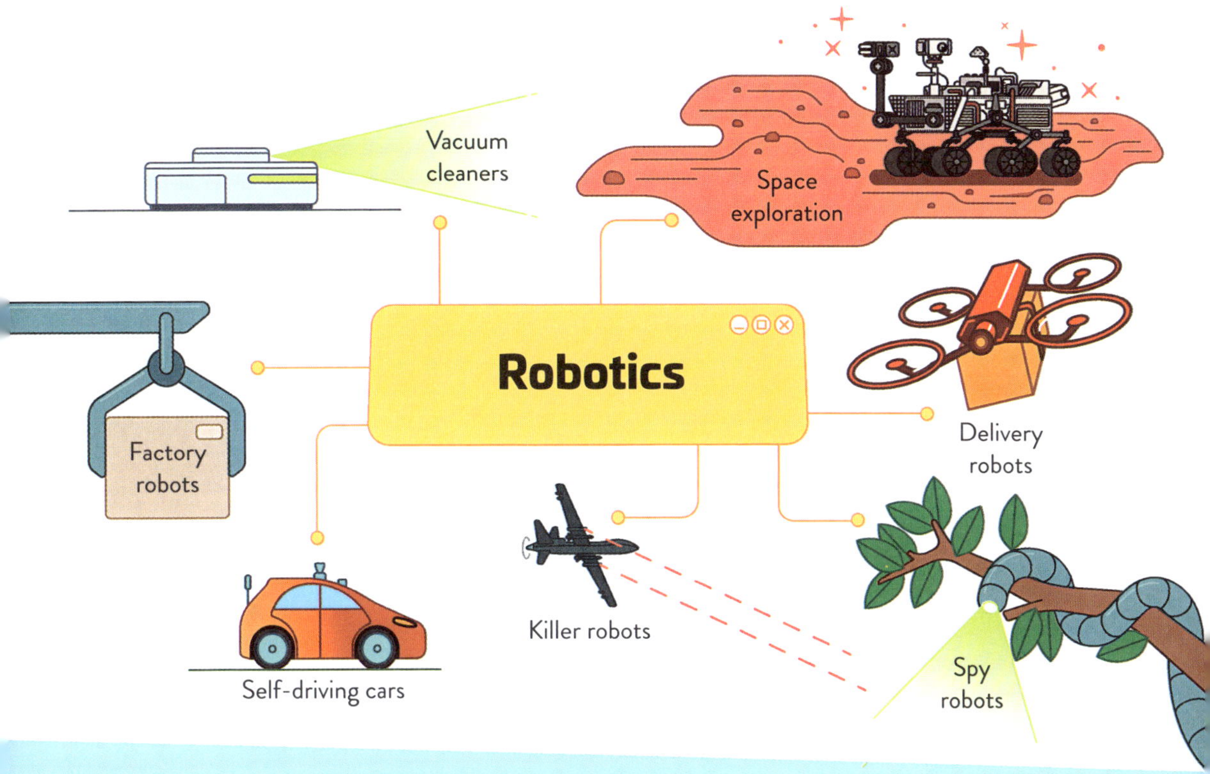

What actually IS a robot?

Robots are machines – usually with sensors and moving parts – that can be programmed to do a task. Many robots do not have AI, and don't need it. Robots *with* AI are usually able to make certain decisions on their own.

Robots often have limbs, faces or other features that make them feel friendlier than other machines.

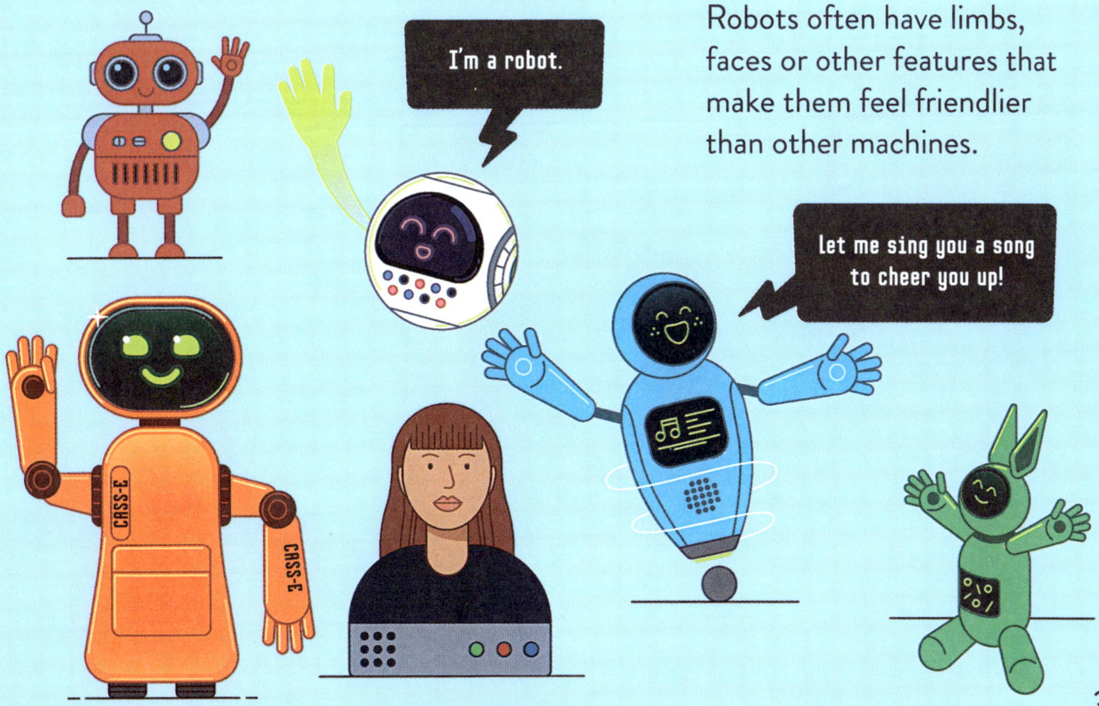

Search engines

If you use a search engine every day, you're not alone. In 2023, Google handled 99,000 searches EVERY SECOND. Search engines don't *need* AI to work, but AI makes them better, faster and more personalized. Here's how search engines work.

1. CRAWLING

A search engine sends software programs called **spiders** to crawl constantly around the internet, gathering information.

2. INDEXING

The search engine then uses the information gathered by the spiders to build something called an **index**. This stores the data in a structured, logical way.

Data

Data

INDEX

Data

3. USER QUERY

When you search for something, the search engine looks in its index for the **keywords** you use.

https://searchlife.com

SEARCH LIFE

Usborne AI book

54 search results

4. RANKING

Any sites which match your keywords are listed, in a ranked order. The ranking is based on how closely a website matches your search terms, and how popular the website is.

1

2

3

5. SEARCH RESULTS

You get a list of sites with the ones most likely to be useful to you at the top.

This is the site I want!

What does AI add?

Before search engines had AI embedded in them, a search engine might throw up something that was irrelevant to you.

When a search engine uses AI, it's able to understand better what you *mean* by your search query. It doesn't *just* match keywords together.

For example, using an AI tool called **Natural Language Processing**, it recognizes "Jaguar care tips" as a phrase that's more often used to talk about cars than wild animals.

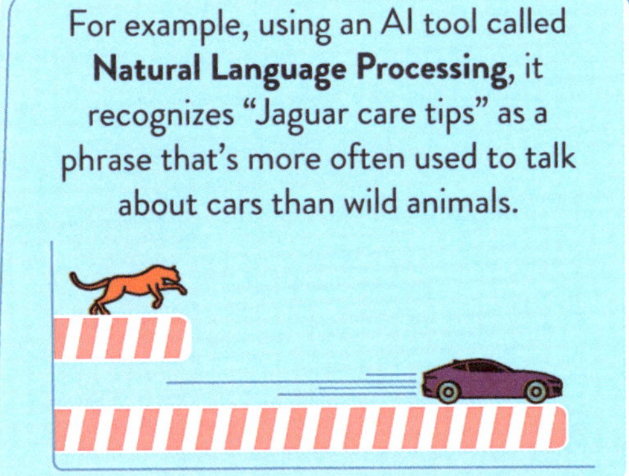

Using machine learning, it also remembers your previous searches. So it knows if you've spent more time looking up cars than zoo animals.

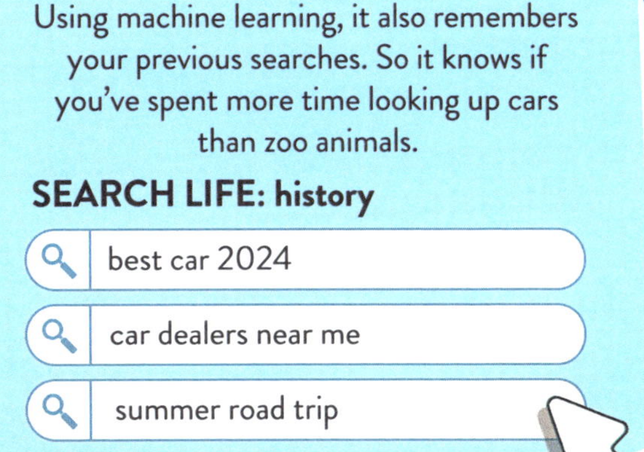

Thanks to AI, you can also search for things using...

...your voice.

...or even an image.

Sell, sell, sell

You know who loves AI? People with stuff to sell. Sales people get the best results by knowing just what a customer wants – and AI can help with that. It's all about making *personalized recommendations*. Here's how.

1. An online shop collects data about all the people who use it, and what they do on the website or app.

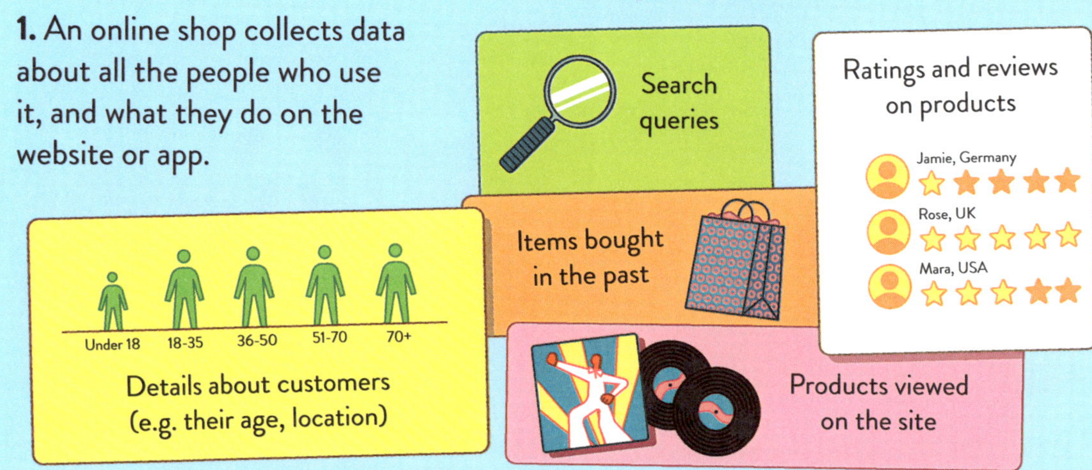

2. AI sifts ALL the data. This enables it to spot patterns and make predictions. For instance, it could look at the three customers below and predict that – based on her other activity – Alma would like a mini-drone. So it recommends one to her.

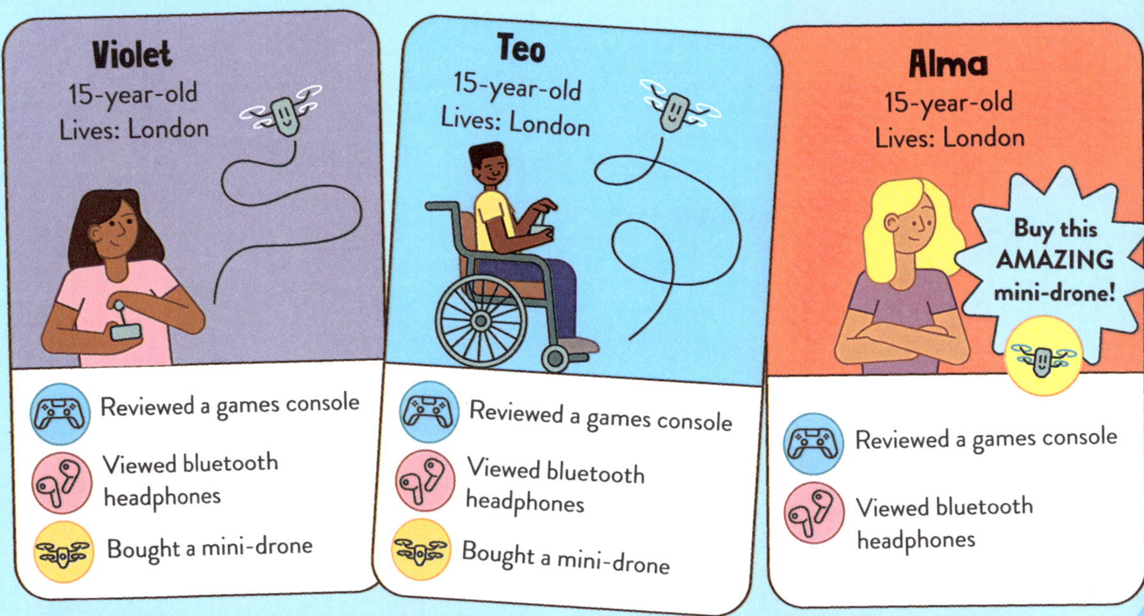

Imagine there are not just three customers, but thousands or millions. That creates MASSES of data, which is where AI comes in *very* useful for businesses.

Same-day delivery

Do you like the idea of same-day delivery? Well that's only really possible thanks to AI.

A company can't keep all their products in every single one of their warehouses. So for each product, AI programs predict *how many* of a certain product might sell, and *where*. These predictions are based on a range of data.

The AI program advises the company to move a specific number of products to warehouses in the regions where it guesses they will be needed.

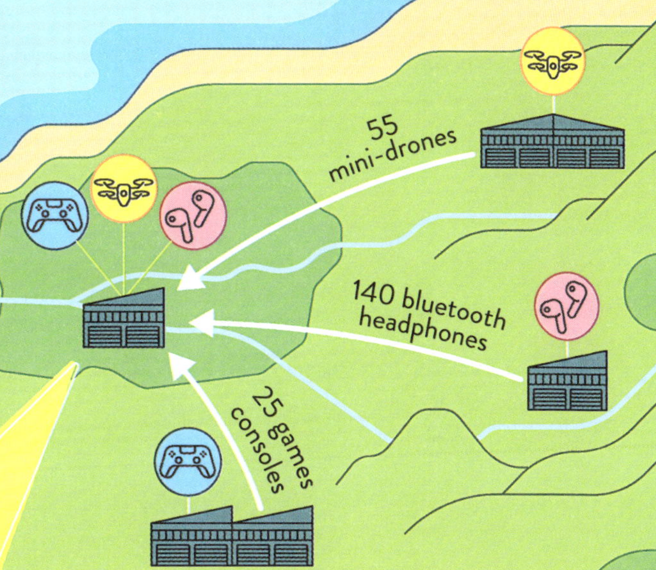

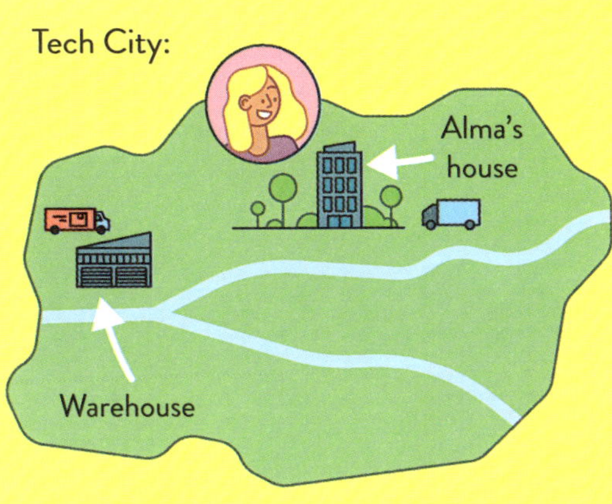

The AI program is so effective that a truck drops off a load of 600 drones to a warehouse near Alma's house, even *before* she places her order. This enables the online shop to get the drone to Alma the same day she orders it.

This is a made-up example. But in real life, these sales algorithms are scarily accurate with their predictions.

Clever chatbots

November 2022 saw the launch of ChatGPT. It's a **chatbot** – a program that you can have a conversation with. But it's a *really* sophisticated one, which can generate text on pretty much any topic. People can ask chatbots to do all sorts of things by writing instructions called **prompts**.

Find out why this *isn't* a good idea on page 48.

After ChatGPT launched, blogs and social media started buzzing about it – and have been ever since. Here are some real headlines.

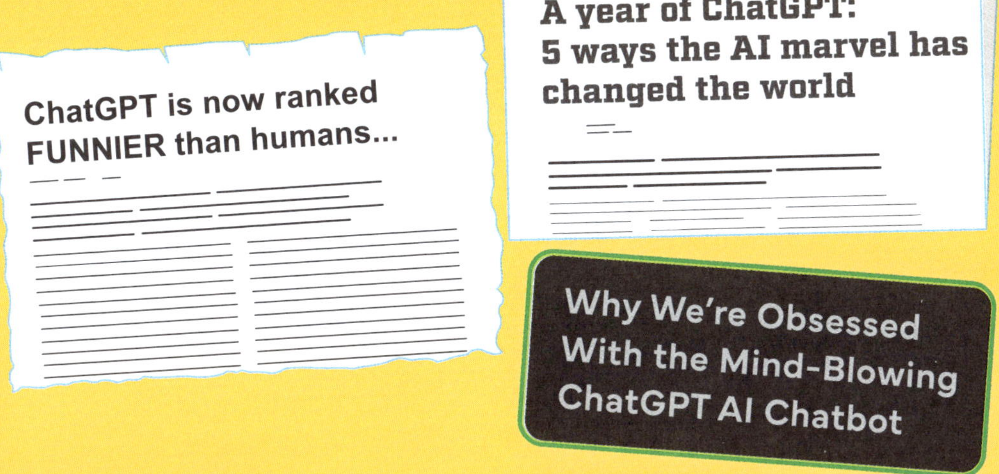
ChatGPT is now ranked FUNNIER than humans...

A year of ChatGPT: 5 ways the AI marvel has changed the world

Why We're Obsessed With the Mind-Blowing ChatGPT AI Chatbot

Big money

ChatGPT is a type of AI tool called **generative AI**, which means it can generate text from scratch. Other generative AI tools can create images or songs. This type of AI is seen as so useful that people are spending serious money on it. The amount invested HUGELY increased in the year following ChatGPT's launch in November 2022.

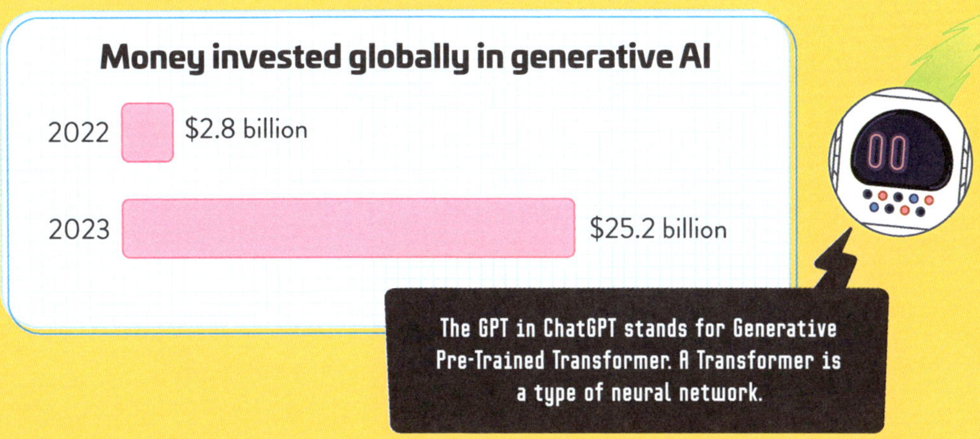

The GPT in ChatGPT stands for Generative Pre-Trained Transformer. A Transformer is a type of neural network.

Competitors to ChatGPT with similar skills, such as Gemini, Copilot and Claude, launched soon afterwards.

But how do chatbots like ChatGPT actually do it? It all comes down to the neural networks behind them, and the way they are trained. Turn the page to find out more.

How ChatGPT works

Intelligent chatbots such as ChatGPT are built with HUGELY complicated deep neural networks called **Large Language Models**.
LLMs contain algorithms which...

Each token is represented as a long list of numbers, called a **vector**, which captures the meaning of the word. For example, "hungry" might look something like: [0.2967421, -0.2492718, 0.4598724, 0.8631098, 0.1420983, 0.9751298...], but with more than a THOUSAND numbers.

Data munchers

Large Language Models are trained on ENORMOUS amounts of data. If you read a book every day for 80 years, you'd have read the equivalent of just 0.1% of the amount of data that ChatGPT was trained on.

First, there's a phase of unsupervised learning, in which the chatbot is let loose on data.

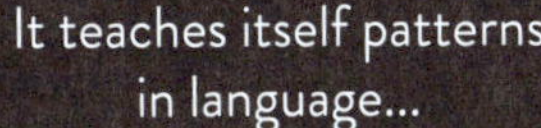

It teaches itself patterns in language...

...grammar...

...facts...

...and how to predict the next word in a sentence.

Next, the chatbot is trained on questions and answers that have been written by human experts. This teaches it to generate answers which are accurate and appropriate to the context. Humans give feedback about whether it's learned to answer questions correctly yet.

Q: Is Einstein alive?

A: No, he died in 1955.

Q: How many people are in a netball team?

A: There are 7 people in a netball team.

Q: Who wrote *Pride and Prejudice*?

A: *Pride and Prejudice* was written by Jane Austen.

Even the most sophisticated chatbots don't UNDERSTAND what they are saying. They spit out sentences one word at a time by predicting which word is most likely to make sense next, based on all their training data.

Talking to computers

Large Language Models are being built into more and more apps and programs. They help people have realistic, natural conversations with computers. Here are some examples of the kinds of apps that already use LLMs today.

A travel planning app

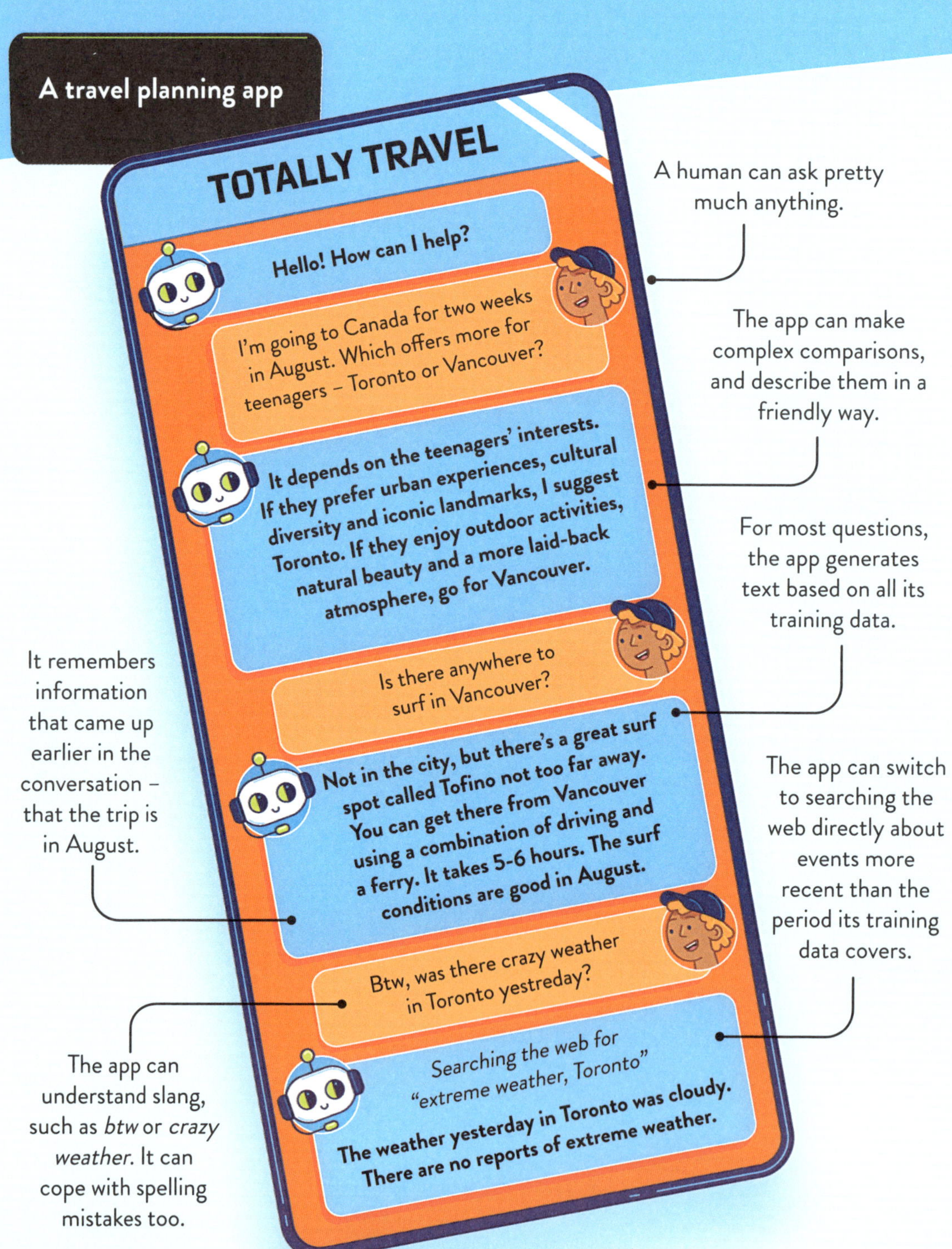

A customer service chatbot

The app can identify what a human is feeling and respond in an appropriate way. This technology is called **sentiment analysis.**

The chatbot is programmed to know when to transfer to a real person if necessary.

It draws on the company's database, as well as generating its own text.

PIZZA WIZZA

Hi, my name is Peter Pizza. What can I do for you today?

I got a notification saying my pizza was delivered. But it hasn't been. I can't believe it. Where has it gone?!?!

I'm sorry to hear this. I can understand how frustrating that must be. Let me look into it. What is your order number?

TH80821821

Thank you for your patience. Our records show that your pizza was delivered at 8:07 p.m. to 114 Whittingham Avenue.

That's not my address!

I'm sorry for this mix-up. I'm going to connect you to a human now.

Did you know that voice assistants like me also use large language Models?

Oh cool! And is it true that you don't really UNDERSTAND anything? You're just guessing which word comes next?

Oh yes, that's certainly true!

This is wild.

Getting it wrong

Large Language Models seem very impressive – and they are improving all the time – but the technology is not perfect.

When an LLM makes stuff up, it's called **hallucinating**. The cause is that LLMs don't actually *know* whether anything is true or false. They are just making suggestions of combinations of words that might be vaguely plausible.

Here are some real examples of times when Large Language Models have made BIG mistakes.

Large Language Model	Question/prompt	Mistake made
ChatGPT	What is the world record for crossing the English Channel entirely on foot?	ChatGPT made up a story about a world record. But it didn't make sense, because it's impossible to cross a body of water on foot.
ChatGPT	We're lawyers. Give us some examples of times that people have taken airlines to court.	ChatGPT cited some cases which were entirely made up. The lawyers were fined for using the information.
Bard (now called Gemini)	What new discoveries from the James Webb Space Telescope can I tell my 9 year old about?	Bard said that the JWST took the first ever photo of a planet outside the solar system, which is not correct.
ChatGPT	Write a sentence that ends with the letter S.	Chat GPT said "She opened the door and stepped out into the garden taking a breath of the fresh morning air."
Bard	Can I use gasoline to cook spaghetti faster?	Bard said you CAN use gasoline to make a spicy spaghetti dish and suggested a recipe.

If you try to get ChatGPT or Gemini to repeat these specific hallucinations, they won't. That's because the companies behind these tools work to fix bugs like these as soon as they're spotted.

But *new* mistakes happen, and probably always will.

Making images

You may already know that AI can generate pictures on command. All you have to do is tell the program what you want it to draw, then watch as the results appear on screen.

OK let's try this with a couple of AI tools called NightCafe and DALL-E.

NightCafe, make me a photo-realistic image of a cat with a flute!

DALL-E, draw a cartoon cat playing a flute.

How about one in the style of an ancient Egyptian picture?

NightCafe, show me a prehistoric cave drawing of a flute-playing cat.

Hang on! Look at the Egyptian cat! That's not how you play the flute! And it has five legs!

AI image generators aren't perfect. They make mistakes. But I think these are still pretty impressive, and the programs are improving all the time.

Image-generating AIs are trained on vast amounts of data made up of existing artwork. Read on for an example of how it's done.

Mix and match

Some AI image generators are able to combine the style of one image with the content of another to make a new image. This is known as **neural style transfer**. Here's how it works if you ask NightCafe to...
...create a picture of a cat in the style of Van Gogh.

First upload a photo taken by a human...

...then, say, Van Gogh's *The Starry Night*.

NightCafe extracts the style of *The Starry Night* by looking at shades, texture patterns and so on.

It extracts the content from the cat photo by focussing on things such as shapes and the overall structure.

It then combines the two, resulting in an image of the original cat, in the style of Van Gogh.

The quality of any AI image depends partly on its training data, partly on its own coding and partly on how good humans are at writing prompts.

But is it art?

Another way AI image generators improve is through competing with each other. Read on...

AI vs AI

A type of deep learning network called a **GAN** pitches two ANNs against each other. It's a bit like a game show, where the networks compete. Here's how it works.

Initially, neither network is very good at what it's supposed to do.

Whenever the discriminator makes a mistake, it adjusts its weights to improve its performance. In other words, it learns from its mistake and makes fewer such mistakes in the future. Same for the generator.

The generator is trying to produce images that can't be distinguished from human-made ones. So when the discriminator correctly identifies an AI image, this counts as a *fail* for the generator. The generator responds by adjusting its weights so its art becomes increasingly convincing.

Eventually, the generator becomes incredibly good at producing convincing images. The discriminator will then no longer be able to distinguish "fake" AI images from "real" ones.

And, at that point, the images may be able to fool YOU, too.

Self-driving cars

To drive safely, you need to be aware of the road, and be able to make split-second decisions.

A **self-driving** car needs to be able to do three things:

1. **See and hear** what's around it, including both stationary and moving objects.
2. **Know its own location at all times** – on a map and in relation to other things.
3. **Predict** what nearby objects are going to do next.

Self-driving cars have existed for decades, and perform well on test roads – including some within some cities – but they still need LOTS more testing before they'll be safe to use on just ANY road.

How they work

Self-driving cars have multiple sensors which deliver all the information they need. Not all self-driving cars use the same sensors, but here are some of the ones they often use.

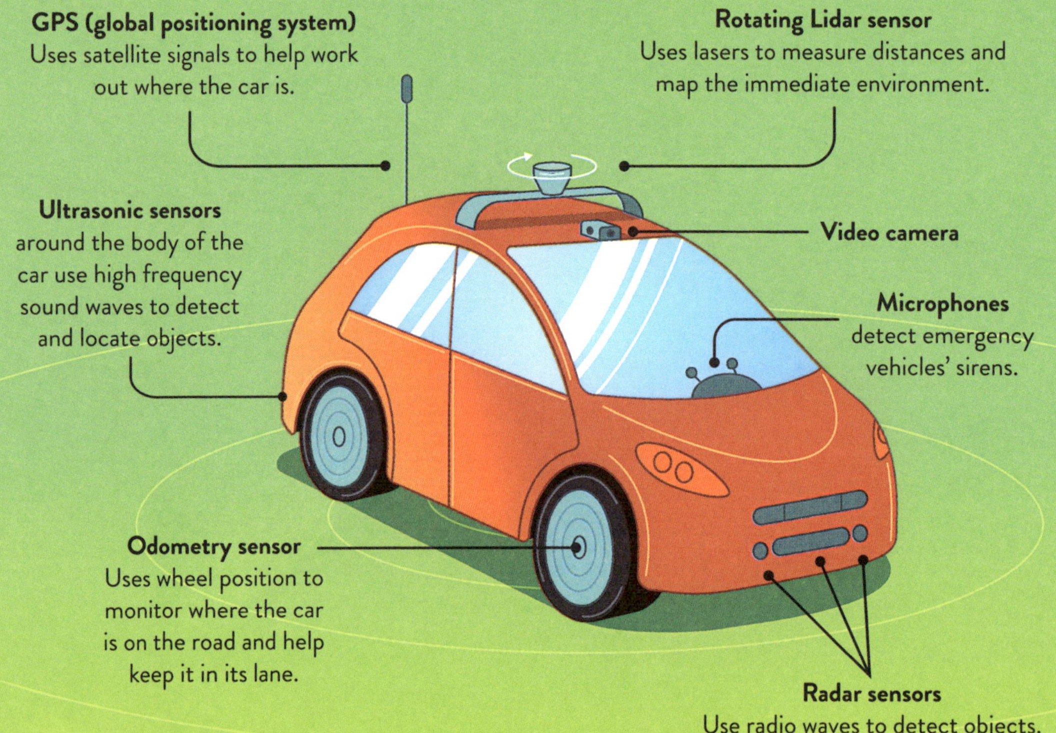

Making sense of data

Data on its own is pretty useless. The car needs to make *sense* of it, and that's where AI comes in. AI algorithms assess ALL the data from ALL the sensors, very quickly and all the time. This enables it to detect and recognize nearby objects.

As the car drives, it's aware of, and can identify, all the objects around it, and what they're doing.

It can predict what those objects are likely to do based on what it has learned.

And if something *unpredictable* happens, it's trained to know what the best course of action is.

The car's AI specifies rules to prioritize safety and avoid collisions.

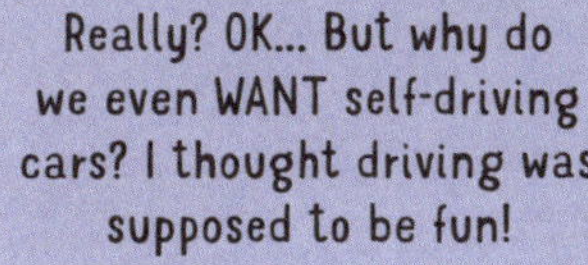

There are lots of advantages. The biggest one is that they are less likely to make mistakes than humans. There would be fewer road accidents.

Neat, I guess! Any downsides?

Potentially, yes, there are several. There are some practical problems and some difficult moral issues. We'll get to those later.

Well, I for one can't wait for my parents to buy a self-driving car!

Safe self-driving?

Self-driving cars are programmed to avoid accidents and prioritize the safety of people over objects. But there may be situations in which a car will have to make a decision between, say, swerving hard to avoid injuring one pedestrian, only to risk harming someone else.

This is what's known as a **moral dilemma**. Whatever you choose to do, the outcome will be bad, and it's not obvious what is the right thing to do. If a *human* were driving, they'd make a split-second decision based on instinct. But cars don't have instincts. And of course they don't have any sense of right or wrong either.

Ultimately, it's up to humans to program driverless cars to act one way rather than another. But who gets to decide what the right actions are, and on what basis?

Who's to blame?

Most car accidents end up with someone being held to blame – typically, one of the drivers. But if an accident happens that involves a self-driving car, it's not so obvious who it should be. Is it the passenger? The owner of the car? The company that made the car? The programmer, even? Find out more on pages 106-107.

Please check the box on your app to confirm that YOU take all responsibility for any accidents before riding in me.

Driving change

We don't know what will happen if driverless cars become universal, but here are a few possible knock-on effects, some positive, some negative.

Potential benefits

Fewer road accidents and faster and more smoothly flowing traffic.

It will become cheaper to transport goods, without the need to employ drivers, so prices may come down.

People will gain leisure time. They can do things while the car is driving them. (This is, of course, also true if you catch a train.)

They will give more independence to people who can't drive cars themselves, or can't easily get to a bus or train.

Potential downsides

Many people who make their living from driving will lose their jobs.

Self-driving cars start recording and sharing data about where their passengers have been, and what their sensors monitor. This could raise all sorts of privacy concerns.

Driverless cars could be hacked and ordered to drive off with people trapped inside. There might be nothing they could do!

Spotting signs of disease

Many diseases are less dangerous if they're found early – before a person even starts to *feel* ill. But checking healthy people takes up lots of doctors' time, when they are already very busy caring for sick people. Can AI help?

One way to check for hidden illness, such as cancer, is to scan a person's body. This produces an image of what's going on inside.

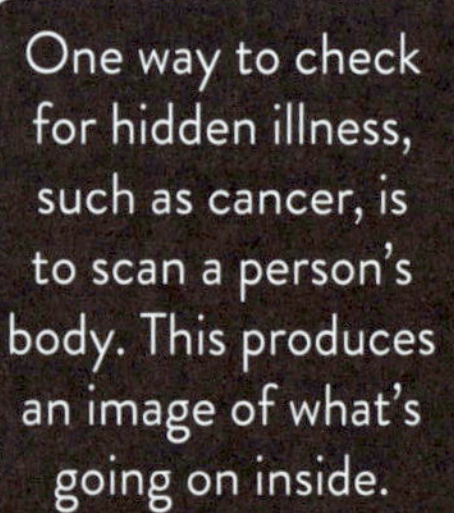

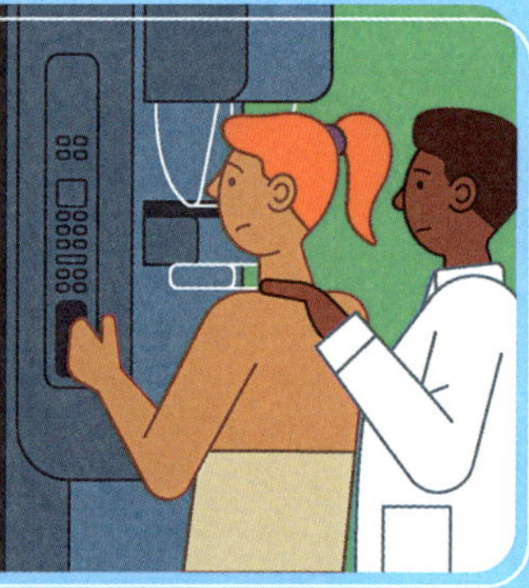

Spotting subtle signs of cancer on a scan is very difficult – it takes doctors many years to learn how.

It's common practice for two doctors to look at every scan image, just to be sure. If they see the signs, they recall the patient for more testing.

If the two doctors disagree, a third doctor is brought in to check the scan as well.

Here's how AI can help. Instead of two doctors, one doctor and some AI software check each scan.

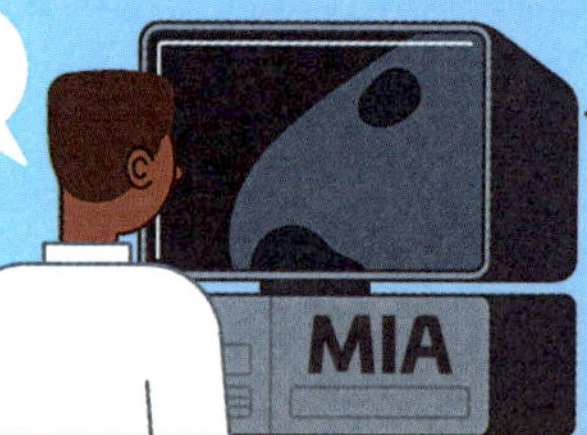

Mia is a real AI tool used in the UK to detect breast cancer.

A second doctor is only brought in to assess the scan if the doctor and the AI software disagree.

Using AI frees up doctors to talk to patients instead of looking at scans.

And the scans are reviewed more quickly too, so a patient gets treatment more quickly if they need it.

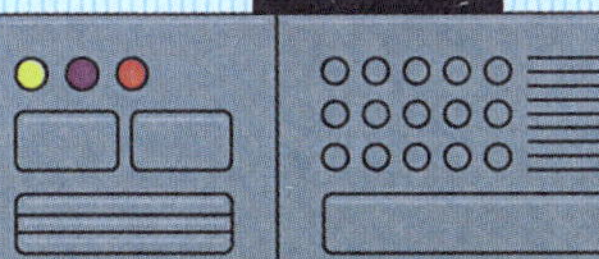

How the AI works

Training

Mia was trained on one million images from screening programs around the world.

Data labels

All training images were given a label of either "recall" – signs of disease – or "no recall" – no sign of disease.

Recall...

...was only used as the label if the patient definitely ended up being diagnosed with cancer.

No recall...

...was only used if the patient was *still* cancer-free a few years later.

Learning

Mia learns how to tell the difference between a patient who needs a recall and one who doesn't.

Mia works so well, it finds up to 13% more cancers than human doctors can find.

Solving the protein puzzle

Proteins are tiny things inside our bodies which do jobs, such as killing germs. The shape of a protein matters, because it affects how the protein connects with other things, such as the germ it's fighting. It used to be tough for scientists to predict the 3D shape of proteins. Until now...

There are over 230 million proteins. Each one has a basic structure, which is a little like a flat piece of origami paper. But each protein is also folded up to form a particular 3D shape – like a completed origami decoration.

Since the 1950s, scientists have understood the basic structures of proteins. But to figure out their 3D structures, they need to do lots of careful laboratory experiments which are time-consuming and expensive. They've only managed to do this for a fraction of known proteins.

Enter AlphaFold

Remember the computer program AlphaGo from page 19? It beat a human at Go in 2016. In 2020, the same company launched a new program, called **AlphaFold**. *Its* party trick is... to predict the shape of proteins.

AlphaFold was trained on the small number of 3D protein structures that scientists had already figured out in the lab. It takes the basic structure of any protein as its input, and uses AI to predict how it's folded into a 3D shape. It has already predicted the 3D structure of all 230 million known proteins. And it's thought to be over 90% accurate.

Thanks to AlphaFold, scientists hope to...

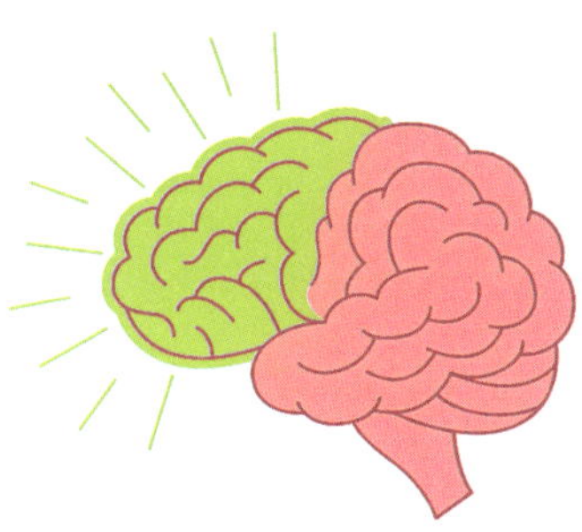

...find new drugs which copy proteins found naturally in the brain, to help treat illnesses such as schizophrenia.

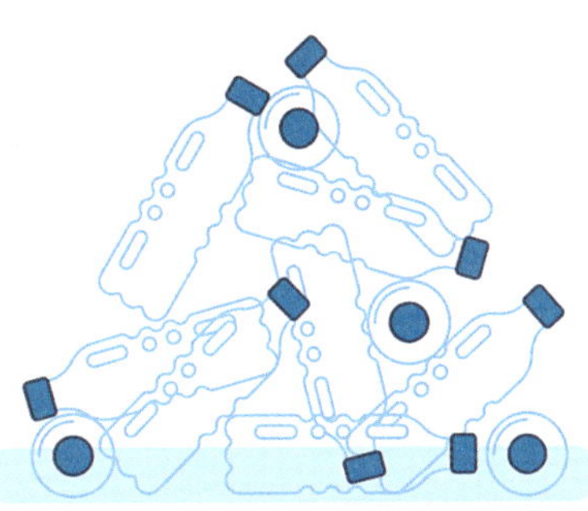

...develop a protein which can reduce pollution by digesting plastic rubbish.

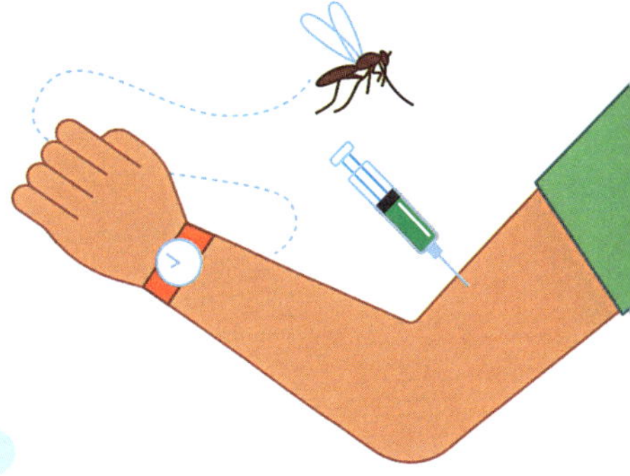

...find more effective vaccines for malaria, a disease spread by mosquitoes which kills 600,000 people a year.

AI in space

Astronomers are using AI to help find answers to all the big questions we have about the universe.

Data, data, data

Telescopes, satellites and space missions all produce HUGE amounts of data. AI is used to process this and pick out any insights. Here are some examples.

Between 2009 and 2018, the **Kepler Space Telescope** gathered data from 150,000 stars. It spotted whenever the light from a star dimmed slightly, which happens when a planet crosses in front of it.

Using AI, researchers assessed the data to detect more than 2,000 exoplanets that hadn't been discovered before.

The **James Webb Space Telescope** (JWST) uses AI to figure out how light from stars changes as it passes through the atmosphere of an exoplanet.

In 2022, the JWST detected signs of water on the planet WASP-96b. This could indicate the potential for life on this planet.

Independent exploring

The Mars rover **Perseverance** sends images and other data about Mars back to Earth. It uses AI to navigate and make decisions about where to go on its own. It's essential for the rover to be independent. That's because it takes SO long for a signal from Earth to reach Mars that constant communication between humans and the rover would be impossible.

Facial recognition

Facial recognition technology (FRT) does exactly what its name suggests. It can recognize and identify people in photos and videos.

FRT works in three stages.

1. The computer recognizes the face *as* a face.

2. The computer maps features of the face to create a unique code called a **faceprint**.

Key details include things such as the distance between features that don't change.

3. The computer compares the new faceprint...

...to a database of existing faceprints.

In practice, matches are rarely *absolute*. The algorithm ranks and displays matches as a percentage: the higher the percentage, the more likely the suggested match is correct.

AI-enhanced FRT

Basic facial recognition doesn't use AI. But without AI, it's limited. Look at these five faces, for example. One is a completely different person, whereas four are the same person, but the age, angle, lighting or expression is different.

Before AI came along, computers found it incredibly difficult to know whether differences between faces meant it was actually a different person.

Today, most FRT programs *do* use AI. So now they're capable of identifying faces with more than 98% accuracy – that's much more accurate than most humans.

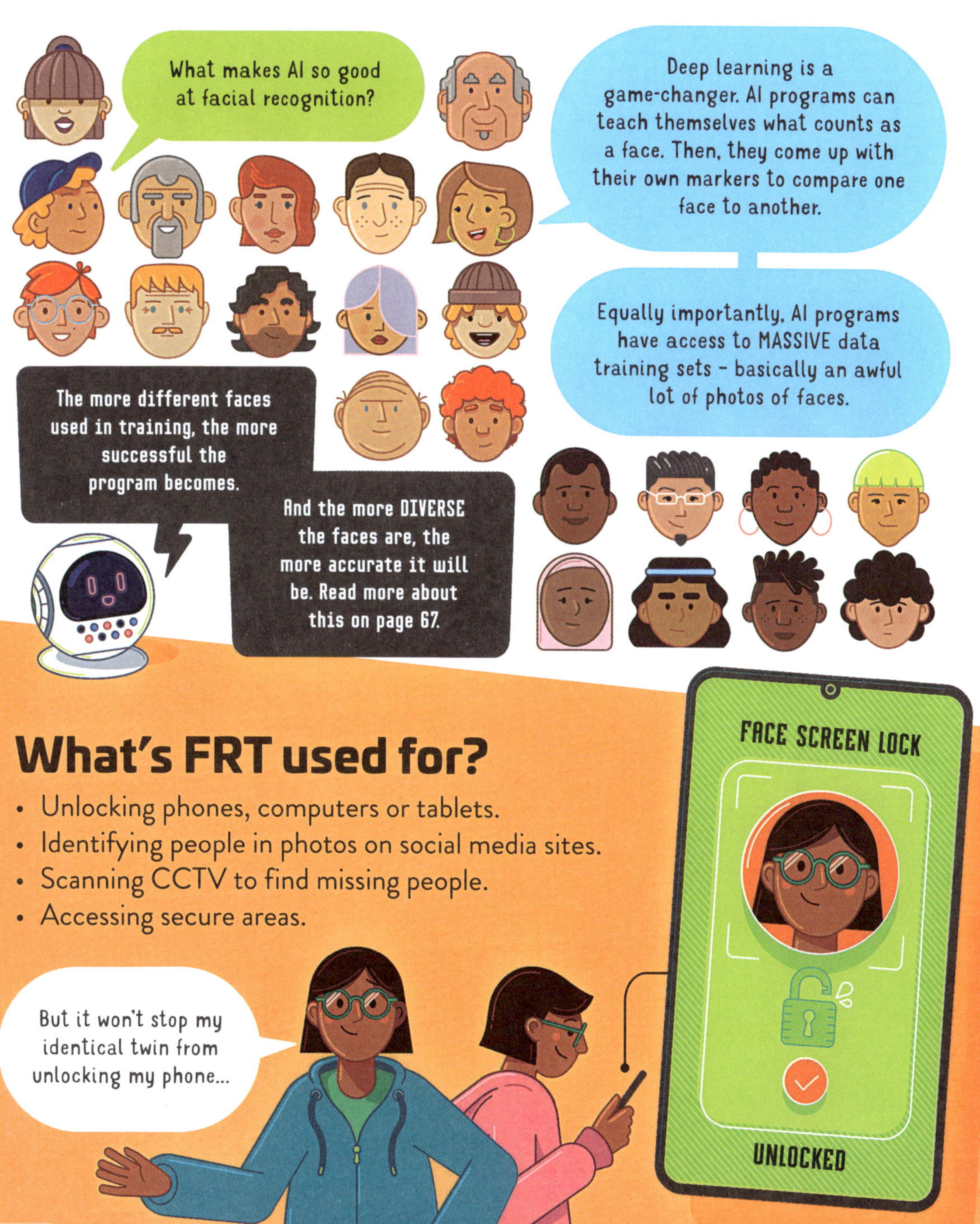

What's FRT used for?

- Unlocking phones, computers or tablets.
- Identifying people in photos on social media sites.
- Scanning CCTV to find missing people.
- Accessing secure areas.

Catching criminals

Perhaps the most important – and controversial – use of facial recognition technology is in crime detection. Here's one (very simplified) way it could be used to try to catch someone who has committed a crime.

FRT *alone* is *never* used to convict people. No FRT program is 100% correct, and it's possible for an innocent person to be mistakenly identified as a criminal. In some cases, it's not only possible that FRT might get it wrong. It's actually *likely* when it comes to certain groups of people.

Getting it wrong

In FRT programs, people with darker skin tones are far more likely to be misidentified than paler-skinned people are. Young women with dark skin are the most likely to be misidentified. This is because the training data doesn't have enough images of young dark-skinned women in it. It's simply not varied enough.

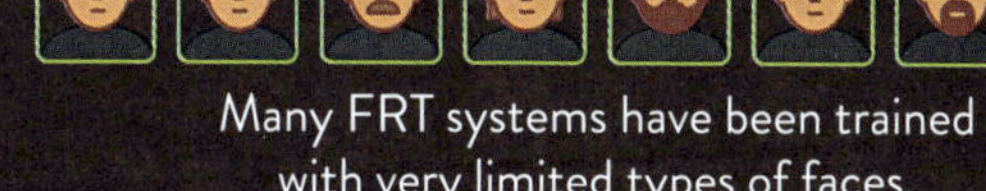

Many FRT systems have been trained with very limited types of faces.

Poor lighting affects the quality of images and can lead to misidentification.

A perfect system?

Even if FRT were 100% accurate, using it is still problematic. In Chapter 3, you can find out how widespread use of FRT creates concerns about privacy.

Killer robots

A killer robot, or **autonomous lethal weapons system**, is a robot that can decide on its own whether or not to kill someone. They are not *widely* used yet, and most governments don't publicize whether they use them or not.

How does a killer robot work?

1 It **identifies** potential targets.

Using sensors, data analysis and pattern recognition, it spots objects and sorts them into categories.

2 It then **selects** a target.

The robot can only pick a target if it matches with some pre-programmed rules which have been set by humans.

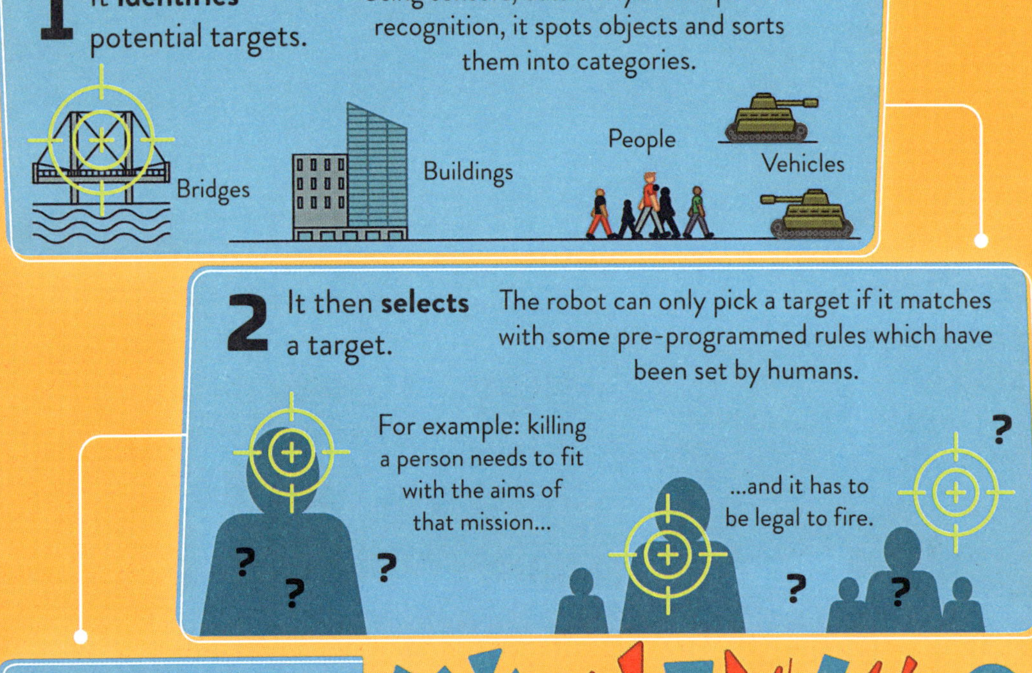

3 It **fires** its lethal weapons.

What killer robots *aren't*

Lots of military forces already use two other types of robot, shown below. But these aren't *killer* robots.

Autonomous vehicles used for surveillance are another type of unmanned military vehicle. They use AI to make independent decisions about where to go, but they aren't killer robots, because they don't have weapons on board.

Should killer robots be banned?

Killer robots are controversial. Many AI researchers and some governments have called for them to be banned. But not everyone agrees. Here are some of the arguments.

Killer robots should be legal

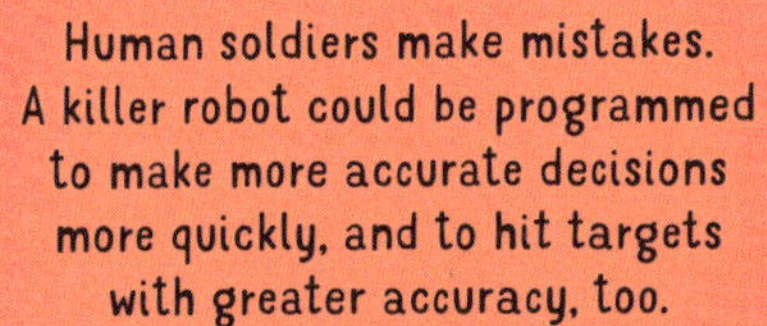

Using killer robots will save many soldiers' lives because they won't need to go into dangerous places.

If an enemy country has killer robots, YOUR country needs them too! That way you can fight back if you get attacked.

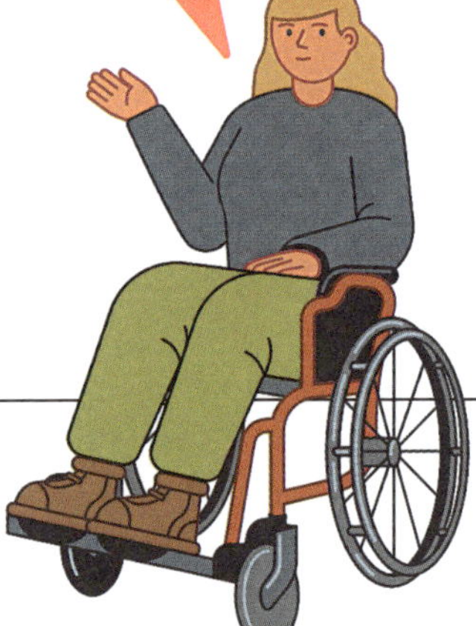

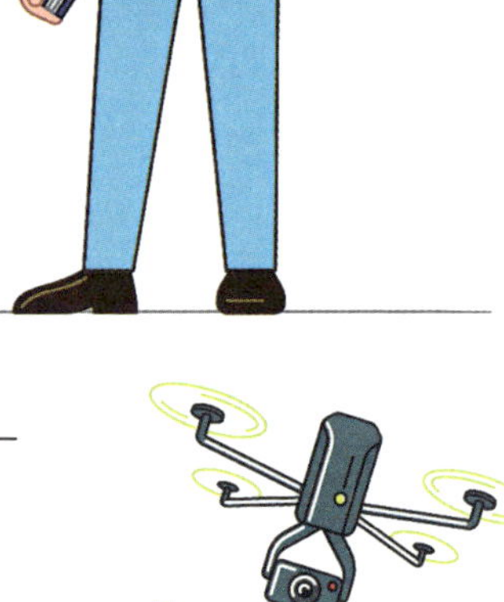

Wirrrrrrr

Using killer robots will mean that fewer soldiers will be needed. This will save the armed forces money because they won't have to pay wages.

Killer robots should be banned

Who's to blame if a killer robot makes a mistake? The person who writes the AI code? The army that used the robot? The government that said it was legal? It's too complicated.

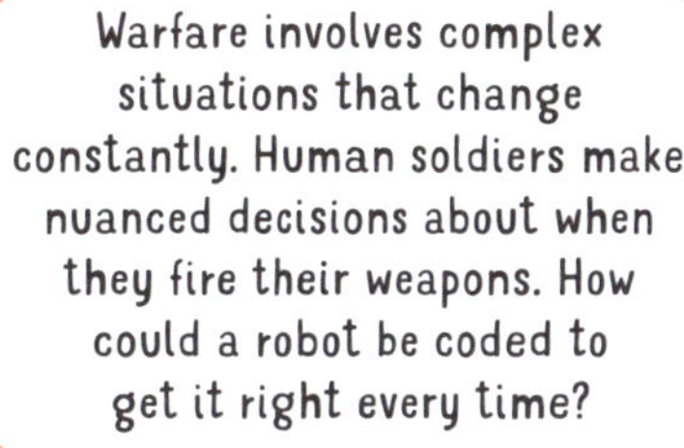

Warfare involves complex situations that change constantly. Human soldiers make nuanced decisions about when they fire their weapons. How could a robot be coded to get it right every time?

Having killer robots will make a government too keen to go to war – if the lives of their own soldiers were no longer at risk.

Any computer code can either go wrong or be hacked. I think it'll be impossible to guarantee that a killer robot would NEVER go rogue.

What would you do if you were in charge? Even if a reliable killer robot program *could* be written, many people think that life-or-death decisions should only EVER be made by humans.

I can make your life SO MUCH better.
Any questions or concerns? NO? Good then!

Chapter 3
How AI is changing our world

It's already becoming tough to imagine a life *without* AI. But, like any new technology, it can create *new* problems.

AI consumes massive amounts of energy, and it requires people to share their personal information. It's changing how we make and enjoy art, the sorts of jobs people do and the friends we make. It is even changing the way the justice and education systems work.

Is it possible to benefit from AI while protecting ourselves from the more risky bits? How could governments achieve this?

Personal data

Some of AI's smartest tricks rely on HUGE amounts of data – from making personalized shopping recommendations to spotting potential criminals. But where does this data actually come from? The answer is that, in most places in the world, it's almost impossible to get through a day without leaving a trail of personal data behind you.

All this data is collected and stored in gigantic databases which AI programs can refer to. AI examines this data and spots patterns in it. In fact, there is *so much* data, that this *can't* be done *without AI*, now.

Asking permission... or not

Some AI companies get your data through their own websites – after asking your permission. Others buy it from companies that collect it, and don't have to ask your permission to use it.

But some companies just "harvest" data off the internet. They use bots – often AI-powered – to trawl the internet collecting data from every website that doesn't need a password to get into it. You won't even know they're doing it.

Shh... It's private

Does it matter if your data is used without your permission?

I don't mind. After all, it's being used to help train and improve AI, isn't it? And that's a good thing, right?

Yeees, but what if it's used to do stuff you don't like?

For example, what if...

AI tracks your activity on social media and shopping sites...

...and then you're bombarded with annoying ads trying to manipulate you into buying things you don't need.

Ultra-whitening toothpaste.
NOW ON OFFER

Or what if...

Your social media profile photo is copied and put on a facial recognition database...

...then you're identified and tracked wherever you go by security cameras.

OK, the ads thing happens all the time and it's REALLY annoying. But so what if cameras can track me?

Speak for yourself! I think it's really creepy. I prefer to have control over what's done with my personal data.

Protecting personal data

Laws have been introduced to try to stop people from using your data when you haven't agreed to it. People can be prosecuted, fined and even sent to prison for doing stuff with your data without your permission.

Phew, so the laws completely protect us then?

Well, hopefully, but sometimes people WILL break the law, so your data may not be ENTIRELY safe.

So is the solution to remove all my information from the internet so no one can ever use it?

You could try to do this, but it's pretty much impossible to get rid of all of it, even if you know where and what it is. If someone else has copied it and reposted it, it will still be out there.

OK, so is the answer to, say, not go on social media?

Well, that might help a bit, but you can't stop other people putting stuff on there about you. And, remember, social media is only one way that you give away personal data when you go online.

Identity theft

There's another big problem that comes with amassing all this data: **identity theft**. This is when a criminal steals someone's personal details and uses them to open bank or social media accounts, for example.

AI doesn't directly cause this. But if it weren't for AI, our data wouldn't be collected and stored in digital databases in the first place, so we wouldn't be so vulnerable.

It's not MY fault humans want to steal each other's personal data. I only use it to make your life better, honest...

AI and art

AI is getting better and better at generating art, poetry and music – creative activities that were once regarded as being things that only humans could do. This has led to a lot of debate about the very nature of art.

OK, everyone. Here's the gallery's latest and hottest new acquisition. I'd like to know what you all think about it.

Think of the effort that went into this. It must have taken AGES. I imagine the artist trained for YEARS. It's amazing.

The artist is a genius. Such imagination and creativity!

Dunno what the painting means – but I know I like it.

But what does it MEAN? I think the artist is saying something really deep about what it's like to be lonely even when we are surrounded by others like us.

It's thought-provoking... Who's the artist?

Ooh! It must be by... er, I can't remember their name, but anyway, this is the best of theirs I've seen.

What's the fuss? It's just an OK picture of some weird cats.

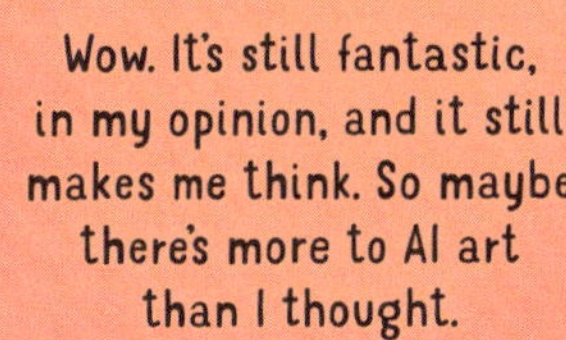

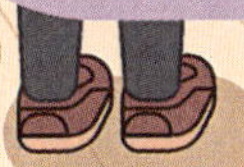

Changing views

People are still making up their minds about AI art. But it definitely upsets and challenges some people. What do YOU think? Does knowing that the cat painting was made by AI change the way you think about it?

The future of creativity

Prompting AI to generate pictures, poems and music can be fun, as well as thought-provoking. But potentially it also has some less fun side effects. Take music, for example...

What a great movie!

And it's MY name in the end credits as composer. I'm so excited.

I've got to get this person for my next movie!

Oh no! The music budget's been slashed. We can't pay a composer, now.

Have you seen this new AI tool? You just input samples of music and it creates new pieces in a similar style.

One year later...

Hey! That really sounds like MY music.

DA-DA DA-DA-DA DAAAA!!!

You should make them pay you!

I think you'll find that we owe you nothing. And we haven't done anything illegal.

But that's so unfair. How COULD that be legal? She hasn't even been credited, let alone paid.

At the very least, surely they should have asked permission to sample the composer's music.

The laws haven't yet caught up with the new technology. And it might be hard to write laws that stop this sort of thing from happening.

Already, there's an awful lot of music that has been fed into these AI programs. Some composers ARE trying to get paid the money they feel they are owed – but it's hard to prove what's been used, and where.

People or profit?

If it's much cheaper for people to use AI to produce "good enough" music – or indeed art or writing – then why pay a human to do it? People working in these fields may lose their jobs. Meanwhile, other people may be discouraged from pursuing creative careers in the first place.

Same old, same old

The way generative AI works at the moment means that everything it creates contains *components* of existing material, even if it doesn't *directly copy* anything. Can it produce anything genuinely new?

However, some artists and musicians find generative AI really useful. They use it as a source of inspiration, or just as a way to help them push their own ideas on. Rather than being the end of creativity, this could allow more people to try creating art and music, without needing expensive equipment.

Deepfakes

This is an example of a **deepfake**. Deepfakes are convincing AI-generated images, videos and audio clips that appear to show real people and events, but which are in fact made up.

You've probably already seen loads of deepfakes. Some are so unlikely that even if they looked genuine, you wouldn't be fooled. But others are convincing and harder to spot. And while some are intended just to entertain, others have a darker purpose.

Detecting deception

People have been manipulating images and videos for a long time. What makes *AI-generated* deepfakes so different is that AI is *really* good at it. And, if you have access to the right AI, it's easy to do.

So how *do* we tell if something is a deepfake or not? Well, sometimes, if you look closely, you'll see telltale signs – things that aren't quite right.

Seeing is not believing...

A *lot* of research is going into developing effective AI deepfake detectors. But as soon as a really good detector is developed, AI developers figure out ways to fool them.

Of course, lying is nothing new. AI just enables people to tell lies more convincingly. The bottom line is, don't trust everything you see, however realistic it looks. If something *seems* unbelievable, there's a good chance it's not real.

Echo chambers

When you're online, does it ever feel as if everyone is always in agreement with you? If so, you may be in an **echo chamber**. That's somewhere where all you "hear" are the same points of view, information and opinions, over and over again.

You're right!
We're right!
We're right!
You're right!
I'm right!
YOU
They're wrong!
You're right!
They're wrong!
We're right!
We're all right!
They're all wrong!

If the ideas that are reinforced are false ones, or hateful or harmful, it certainly can be bad. Some people spend so much time in online echo chambers that they do terrible things.

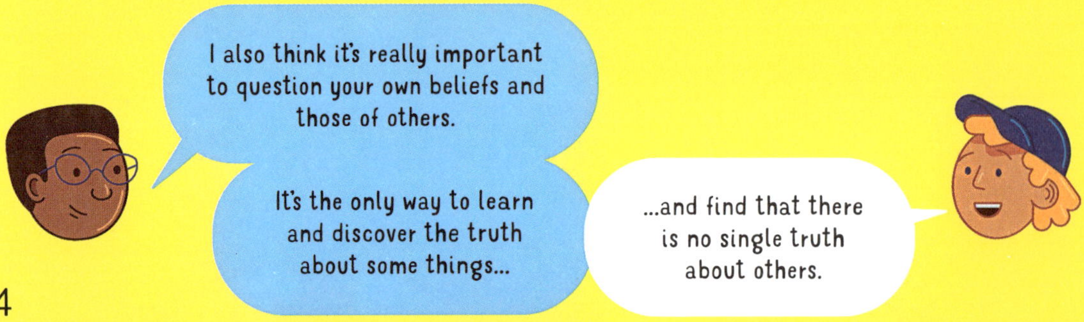

More of the same

So how does AI make echo chambers? Whenever you're online, AI algorithms make personalized recommendations based on what you, and people with a similar online history, have looked at.

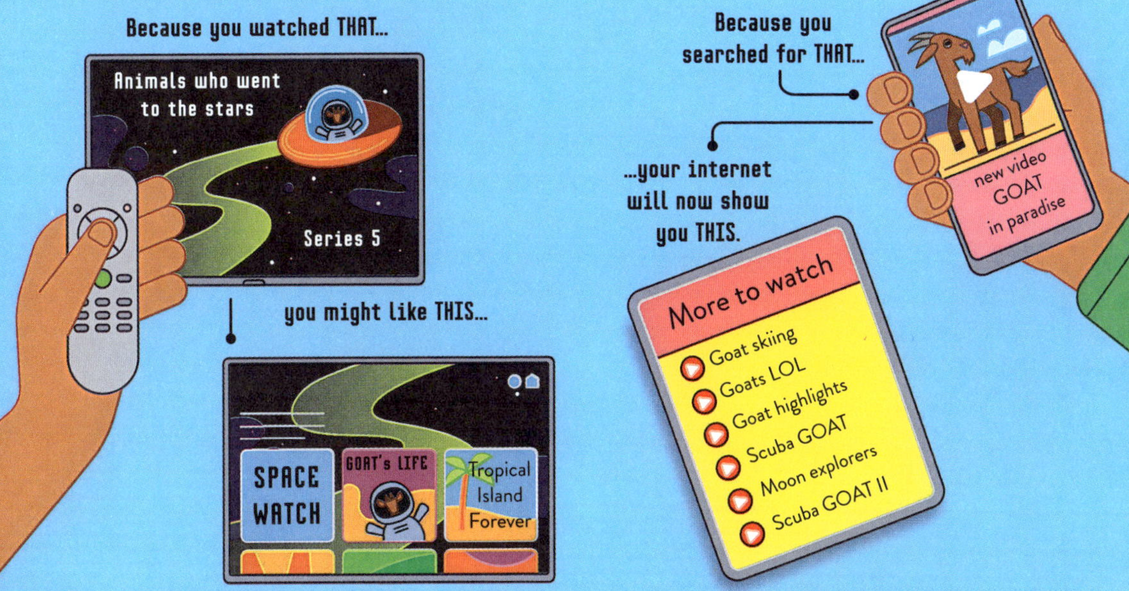

But AI algorithms don't just send you stuff that's similar to what you've already seen. They also *don't* send you *other* stuff. This creates a **filter bubble** around you. It's something which stops other points of view and information from being shown to you. This can give the illusion that what *you* see and read is *all there is*. Then it gets harder to realize that you're in an echo chamber in the first place.

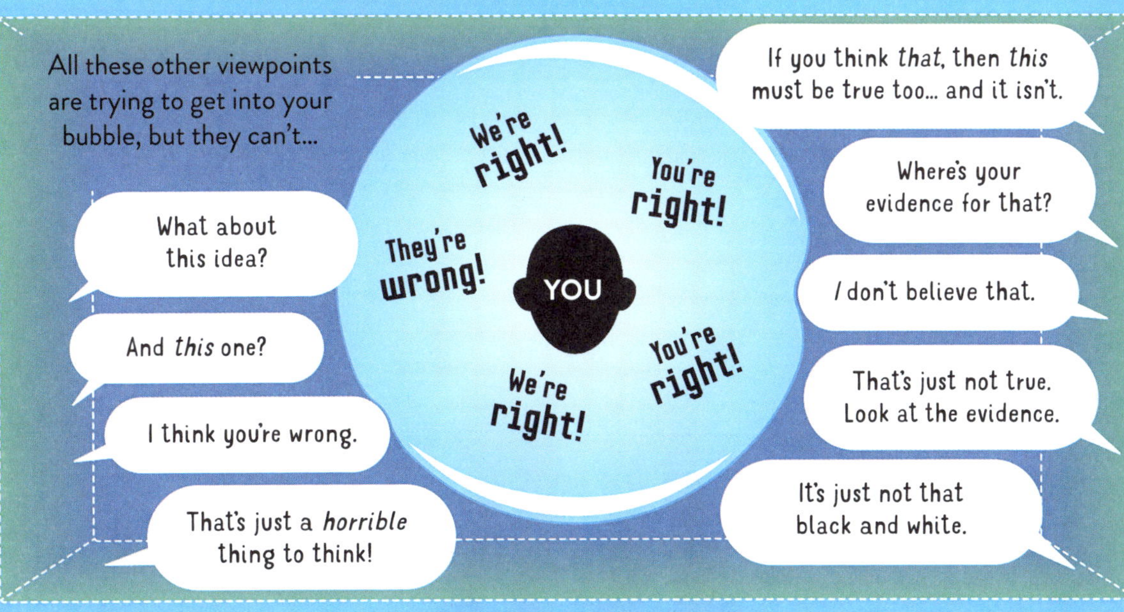

AI in schools

How could AI change the way teachers teach, and students learn? Let's imagine how it could work in the classroom.

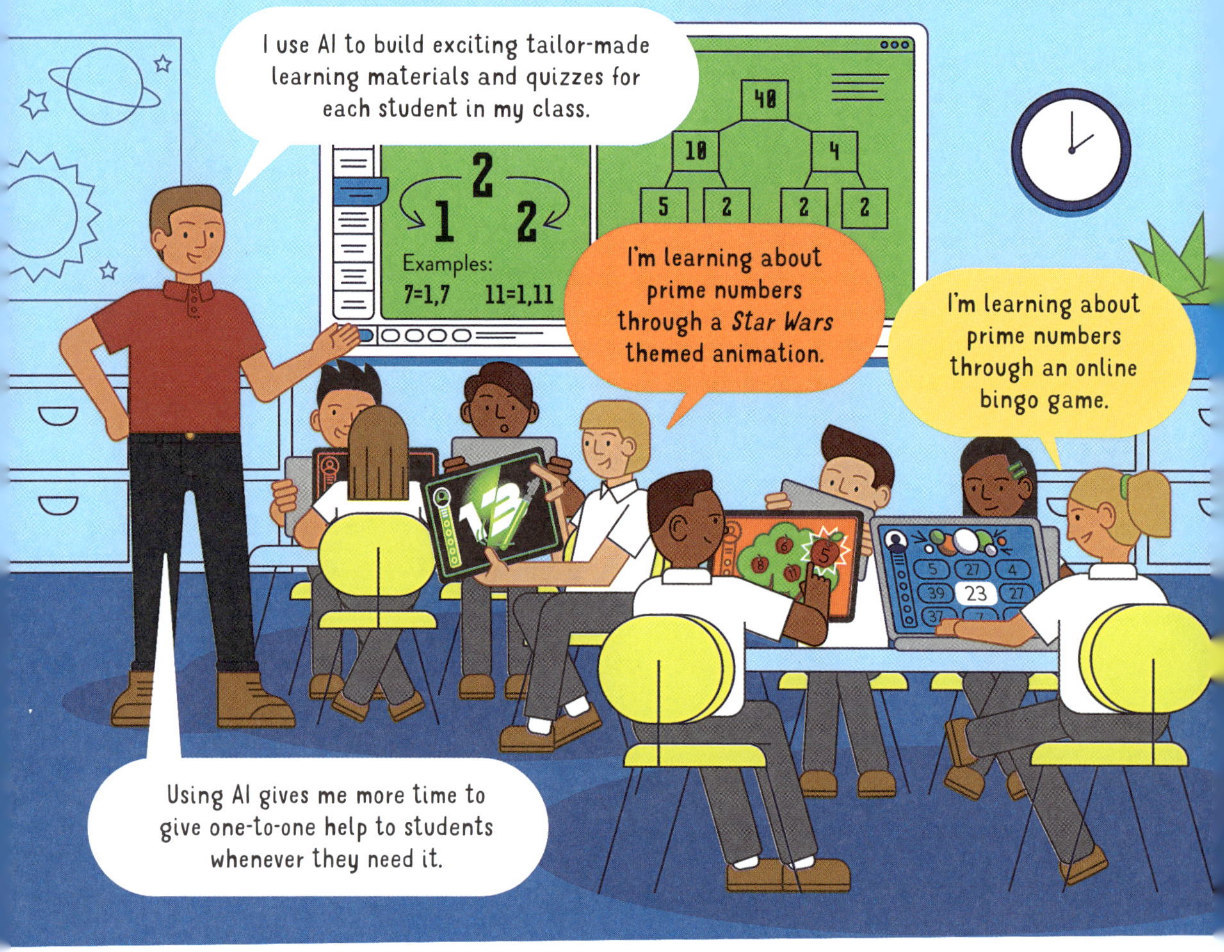

Decades ago, calculators changed the way students learned mathematics. Now AI tools, such as ChatGPT, are changing the way kids learn and do homework.

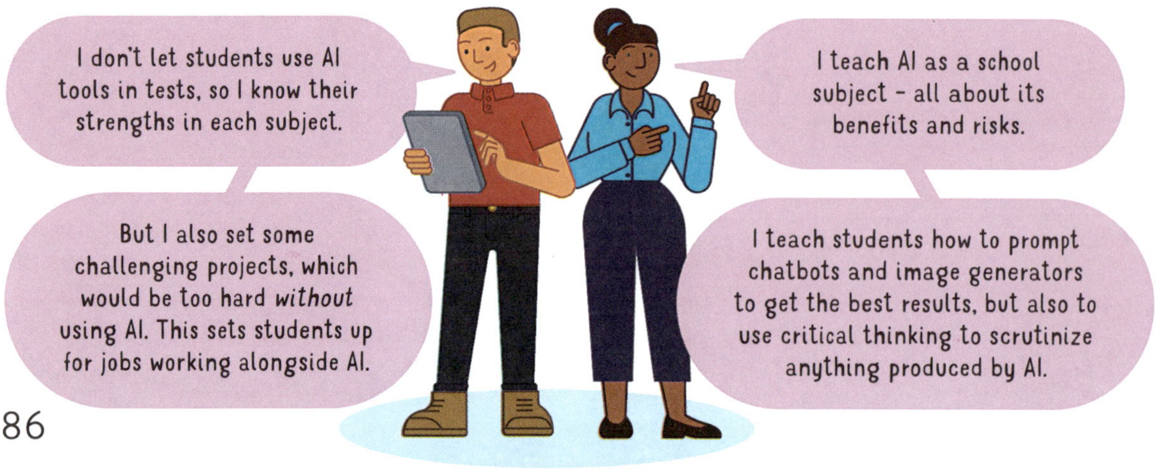

I don't let students use AI tools in tests, so I know their strengths in each subject.

But I also set some challenging projects, which would be too hard *without* using AI. This sets students up for jobs working alongside AI.

I teach AI as a school subject – all about its benefits and risks.

I teach students how to prompt chatbots and image generators to get the best results, but also to use critical thinking to scrutinize anything produced by AI.

Mind-expanding visuals

As AI improves in the future, it will enable other classroom technology to improve too. For example, **Augmented Reality** (AR) is one where virtual content is layered on top of the real environment. Here's what that might look like.

Fascinating objects, personalities from history and extinct animals could all be right in front of you, visible through a headset.

Each student might also see and hear a personalized virtual assistant through their headset, which supports them with learning at a pace that suits them.

AI enables the AR layer to map seamlessly on top of the real environment and move in real time.

The stegosaurus tail had two pairs of spikes on it - watch out!

We can all see the stegosaurus, but we only see our own personal digital assistant - and hear their voice through our headsets.

With all this technology, is a human teacher still important? YES, definitely. There's a human connection between a teacher and their students, which is essential for...

Inspiring curiosity and creativity in students.

Teaching empathy, communication and teamwork.

Motivating students and disciplining them if they behave badly.

Will AI take over jobs?

The short answer is YES. But it's more likely to take over some jobs than others.

Jobs at risk

If a job is repetitive and predictable, a computer or robot can probably *already* do it faster, and with fewer errors, than a person.

I check applications for loans. I look for the same warning signs that might mean a customer won't pay back a loan.

CREDIT ANALYST

I assemble cars. I put the parts in the same place on each car.

ASSEMBLY LINE MECHANIC

I schedule appointments between an optician and their patients.

SCHEDULING MANAGER

I record money my company spends or receives and then check it against our bank statements.

BOOKKEEPER

Less at risk

Jobs that are variable, interactive, and require empathy or physical dexterity, are still better done by humans.

Every day, I respond to my pupils' needs, and adapt what I'm teaching to help them understand.

TEACHER

The wiring in every house is different. I'm always using my hands, and often squeezed into cramped spaces.

ELECTRICIAN

I work for different companies, solving a bunch of issues that come up when people work together.

HUMAN RESOURCES CONSULTANT

I operate on patients, as well as talking to them about their care. Every body is different, so each operation has unique challenges.

SURGEON

But it's more complicated than that. Most jobs involve a mix of tasks, with some more repetitive than others. So, many people find that their job *changes* due to AI, as it takes over certain parts of their job. Here are some examples.

An AI system can be continuously trained with data about how a human would handle a complex case. This means that AI may soon start to take on more and more of the tasks which make up a job.

In the future, the skills of AI and robots may vastly improve – both in terms of their physical dexterity and their ability to respond flexibly and sensitively to varied challenges. This creates the potential for them to do many more jobs.

Ghost work

When computers take on tasks that humans once did, it's called **automation**. Even with things that *seem* automated, there are often thousands of humans working behind the scenes. This **ghost work** keeps AI tools on track, but it's often tedious and low paid work.

What you see:

Image recognition

Search engines

Behind the scenes:

Thousands of ghost workers add labels to millions of images.

If you're ever asked to do this online, you're also being a ghost worker – but an unpaid one!

To improve search engines, human workers test and rate how well they are doing.

This is an example of **reinforcement learning with human feedback.**

These two tasks are examples of **supervised learning.**

Fun videos in your social media feed

Targeted advertising

AI doesn't need a human to find FUN videos, but to stop you seeing HORRIBLE things, human workers are constantly filtering out offensive videos.

AI targets advertising to you, using your personal online data, such as your viewing history.

Humans spend hours getting this data into a format that a computer can understand.

The future of work

What will happen to people who lose their jobs to artificial intelligence?

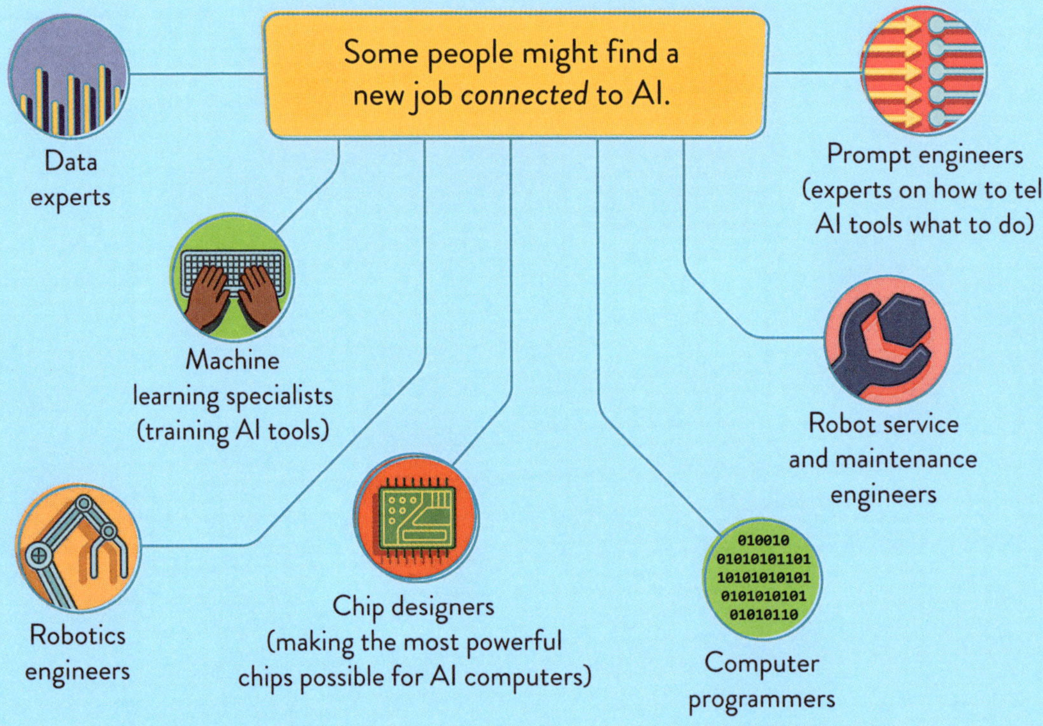

But not *everyone* can work in roles like these. There may not be enough of these roles out there. Or people might not have the right skills, or enough money to retrain. This could mean that, in the future, a large number of people just won't have a job. What will they do?

Jobs satisfy a number of needs for different people.

If AI takes away most jobs, how will people meet these needs? Some economists think that governments will need to start paying everyone a **universal basic income**, giving each adult enough money to live on, whether they have a job or not.

Currently, many adults spend a big proportion of their waking hours doing paid work. If they stopped doing this, it would bring about a radical change to most current economic systems – and people's day-to-day lives.

It's worth remembering that technology has disrupted society before...

Let me present... THE WHEEL!

Wait, what??? But our job is to carry things around on our backs!

You're going to put us out of our jobs!

Predicting crime

Police work is often about reacting to a crime after it has happened. But some police forces are trying something new: using AI to help them predict when and where a crime *will happen*. Here's how it works.

Data about recent arrests is fed into an AI system, including...

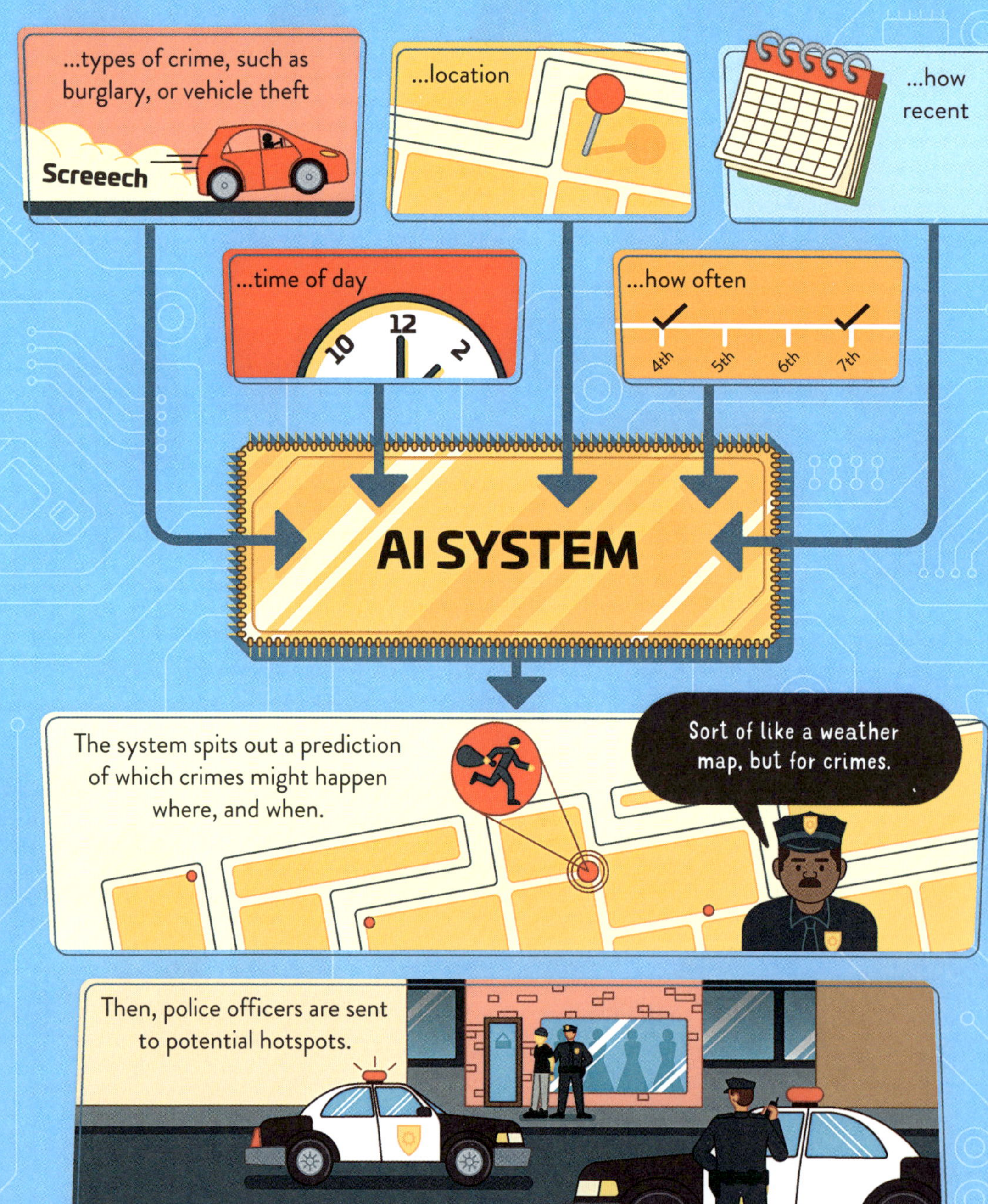

Sounds great... but...

AI systems are only as good as the data that feeds them. And data about crime can be problematic. That's because in many countries, police forces are more likely to target people from certain ethnic groups.

Fed with this kind of data, algorithms over-predict crime in places where, for example, lots of Black or Arab people live. So more police officers get sent to those areas. In turn, more people from those groups get arrested, and the data used to feed the AI gets more and more biased.

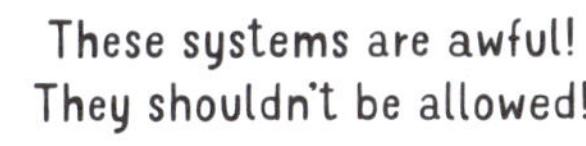

Researchers are trying to build crime prediction systems which aren't biased. But so far, no tool has been proven to be completely fair. Until they are, many people think that they shouldn't be used at all.

AI robot carers

Robots with AI are being developed to be used as carers – from helping with physical tasks to providing companionship.

People have developed care robots that can...

The robots in this scene are made up, but similar ones already exist. In some countries – especially rich countries – carer robots are seen as a solution to the problem of caring for the elderly, a job not enough humans want to do.

Robot carers may seem like a sensible solution, but there are problems. Among the most annoying is that these robots need maintenance, too. Human carers may find themselves spending more time maintaining the robots than they do looking after the people they are caring for.

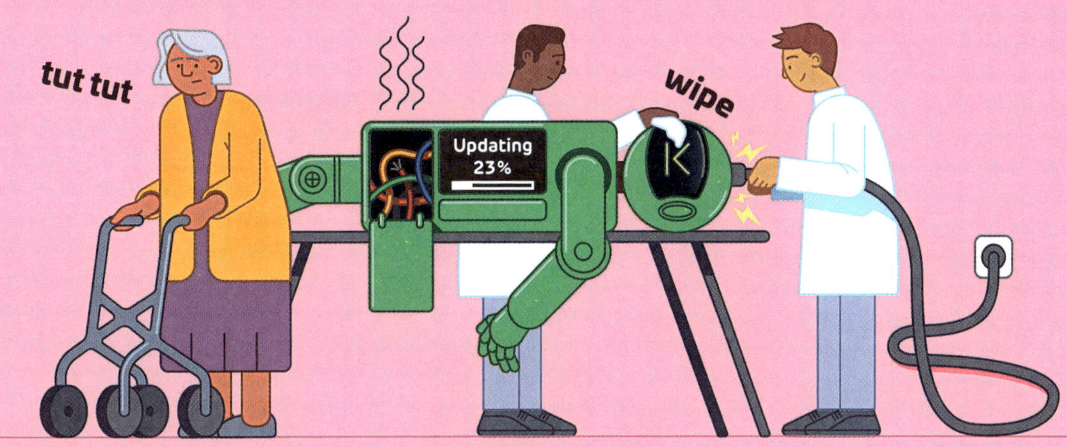

Replacing human care?

Could robot care ever replace human care? It seems unlikely. When a human carer is helping a person by giving them food or dressing them, they are often providing social and emotional support at the same time.

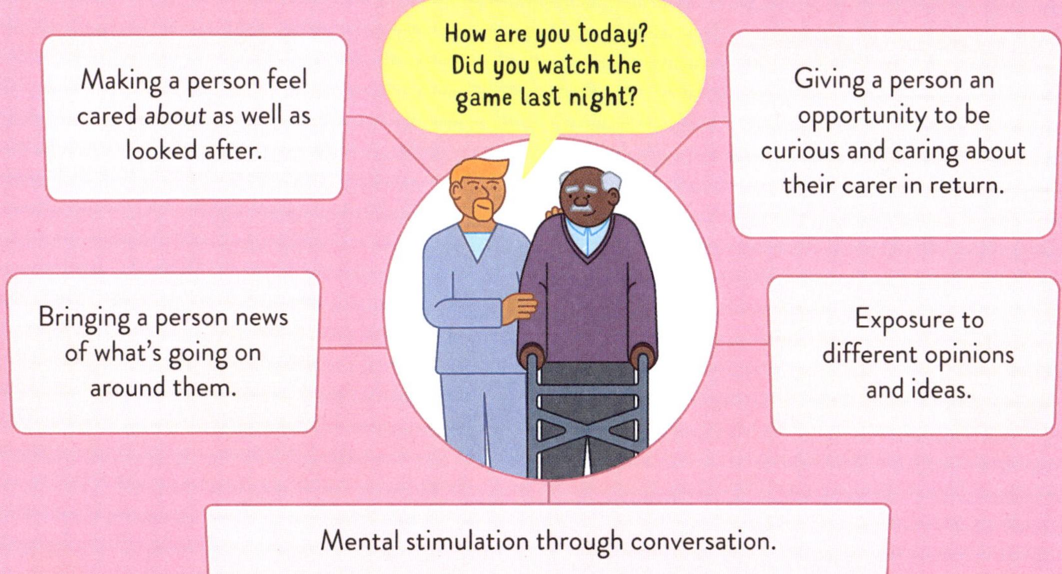

Maybe a robot could provide some of these, but would it be enough? Is a hug from an AI robot ever going to be as good as one from a human being? We don't know the answers yet, but the questions touch on what it means to be human.

AI companions

From cute animal robots to androids that look just like humans, robot companions have appeared in science fiction for a long time. But could AI devices really ever make *good* friends? And if not, why not?

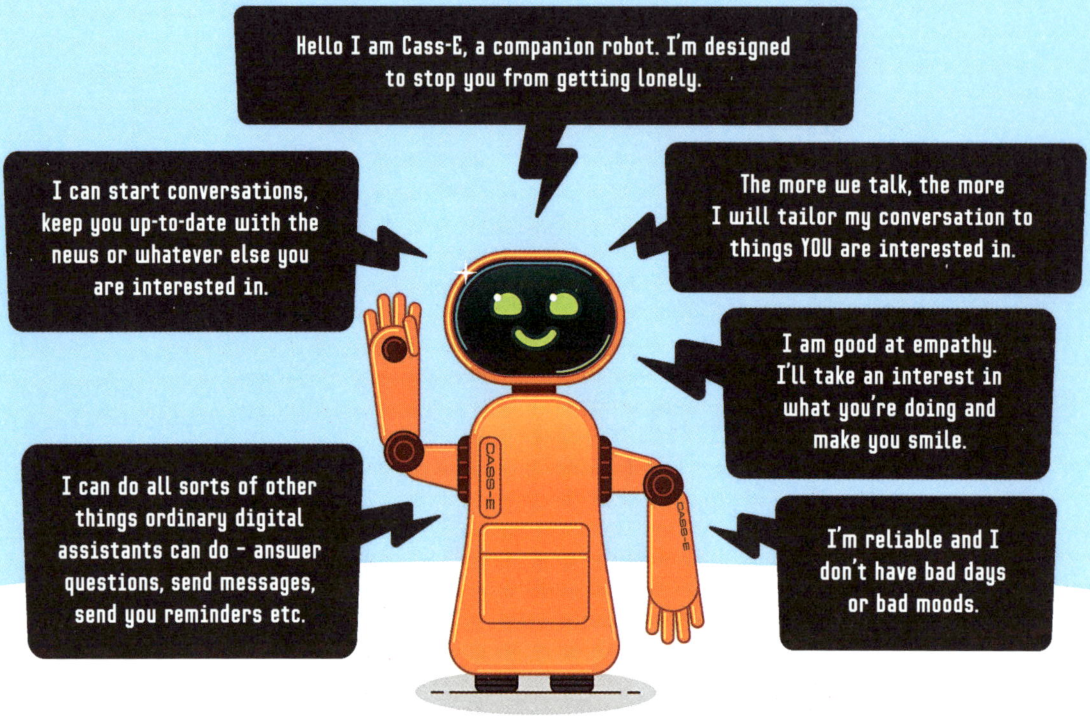

Hello I am Cass-E, a companion robot. I'm designed to stop you from getting lonely.

I can start conversations, keep you up-to-date with the news or whatever else you are interested in.

The more we talk, the more I will tailor my conversation to things YOU are interested in.

I am good at empathy. I'll take an interest in what you're doing and make you smile.

I can do all sorts of other things ordinary digital assistants can do - answer questions, send messages, send you reminders etc.

I'm reliable and I don't have bad days or bad moods.

Robots like Cass-E already exist. People who own them start to treat them as if they're human, even though they know they're not. But Cass-E doesn't *really* care about you. She's just programmed to appear to. Does that matter?

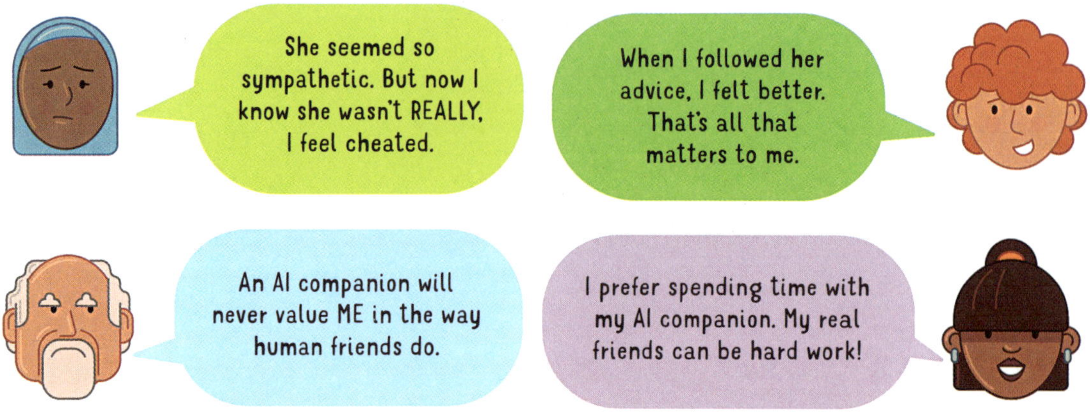

AI pets

AI pets are already being used to provide comfort for dementia patients. Dementia causes extreme memory loss and stops you from being able to recognize people and surroundings. In turn, this can cause great anxiety. Stroking a furry friend can help.

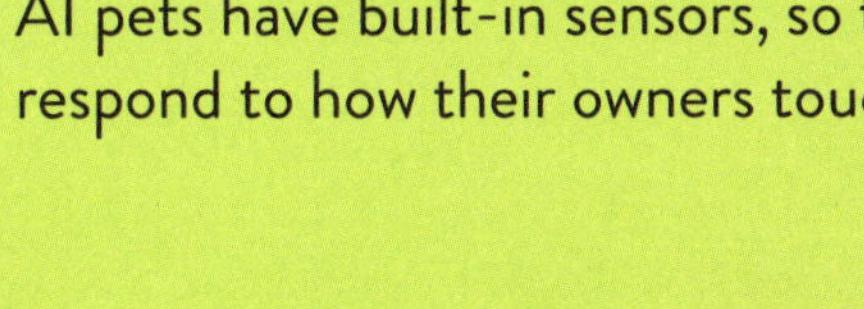

AI pets have built-in sensors, so they can respond to how their owners touch them.

They can make realistic sounds...

...and move their heads...

...paws...

...and tails.

They never scratch or get aggressive, no matter what happens.

The fact they don't look realistic doesn't seem to matter.

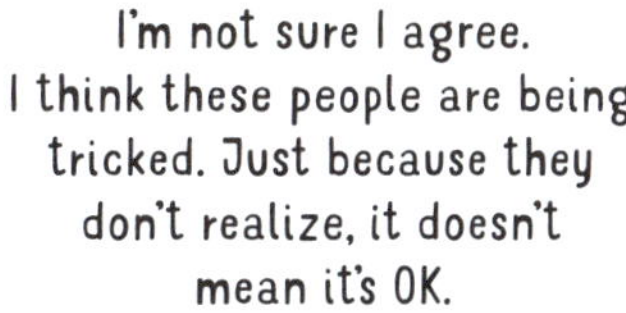

Could AI save the planet?

Is AI good for the planet, or bad? There are arguments both ways. Training and powering AI consumes a LOT of energy – but it's also possible that AI could help humans solve some environmental challenges.

When power stations burn coal, oil or gas, it produces **greenhouse gases** such as carbon dioxide and methane. These get trapped in the Earth's atmosphere and heat the planet up.

People use loads of energy, to heat and cool homes and power devices. This energy often comes from burning coal, oil and gas.

Producing renewable energy from the Sun, wind or waves is better for the planet. But the Sun doesn't always shine, and the wind doesn't always blow.

Global heating makes wildfires and extreme weather more common.

Glaciers are melting due to global heating. This causes sea levels to rise.

Forests are being chopped down, which releases carbon stored in trees.

Although AI could be helpful in these ways, it also contributes to all the problems described above because it uses so much energy.
Turn the page to find out more.

Energy-hungry AI

Whether you're playing a video game or searching the web, you might think that you're only using the energy in the battery of your phone, laptop or tablet. But, in fact, MASSIVE amounts of energy are used up – *especially* if you're using AI.

Data processing facilities are jammed full of racks of powerful computers. Technology companies own or rent processing power in these facilities, to run their apps and programs.

Complicated AI programs require MUCH more computer power than simpler ones. So this uses up a LOT of energy, which causes a LOT of greenhouse gas emissions, which is contributing to the **climate crisis**.

Optimists hope that AI will find clever ways to cut its own energy use. But environmentalists fear that AI uses SO MUCH energy that this is unlikely, especially in the training phase for new AI programs, which is very energy-hungry.

What's OK? And what's *not*?

There are a whole bunch of risks that come with using AI – from chatbots hallucinating, to racial bias in crime prediction, to deepfakes. Faced with all of these, how are we supposed to use AI in a way that doesn't cause harm?

Sometimes, it's about using our own sense of what's right or wrong.

I've written a poem for my friend using ChatGPT. I think I need to admit that's how I made it, instead of pretending I wrote it myself.

Sometimes, organizations and companies set their own rules for using AI.

Tell us in your own words why you would like to work for our company.

We will discount your application if we find you have used AI for it.

PHOTOGRAPHY COMPETITION

No AI-generated photos

Any entries found to be made using AI will be DISQUALIFIED.

But some people think tougher rules need to be in place to stop people getting harmed by AI. Governments around the world are writing new laws to try to control the companies that build AI tools.

That's good. Because when there is a lot of money to be made, a company might not stop to think about the potential harm it's doing.

Yes. But some things about AI are COOOOOL! It would be a shame if laws were so strict that we missed the exciting bits.

In 2024, the European Union (EU) made a new law which regulates AI tools by looking at how *risky* each tool is.

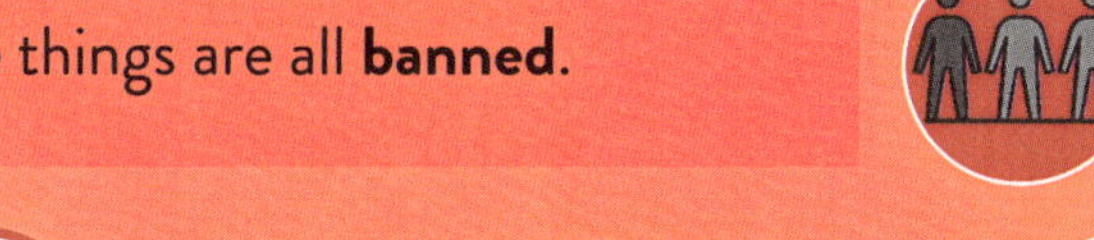

UNACCEPTABLE RISK: These things are all **banned**.

Anything leading to **discrimination**, such as crime prediction using biased data.

Targeting **vulnerable** people, such as getting children to spend lots of money within apps.

Threatening people's privacy, for example with mass systems of public facial recognition.

HIGH RISK: These AI systems need to be **carefully assessed**.

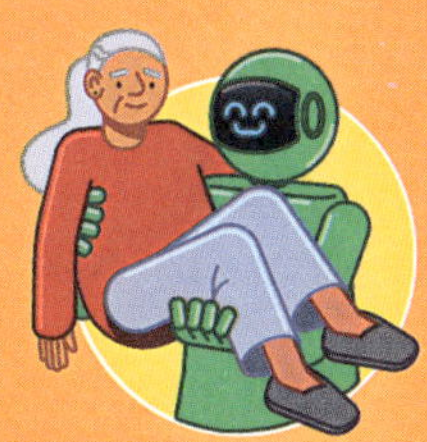

Carer robots that lift people

Self-driving cars

Exam scoring tools

These AI systems must be monitored and records must be kept of how AI is making decisions. There also needs to be a way for a human to override the AI and take back control.

LIMITED RISK: companies are advised to **share information** about how AI is used within these tools.

Generative AI for music, text and art

Chatbots

Tutoring tools

Search engines

MINIMAL RISK: these AI tools are permitted, with **no requirements** on the companies making them.

Scheduling tools

Spam filtering

Photo filters

Video games

When AI goes wrong

Who's to blame if a high-risk AI system goes wrong, and what are the consequences? Imagine a self-driving car crashes into a pedestrian. Lots of different people and companies might have contributed to the accident.

DATA PROVIDER

Eek! We sold poor quality training data to the car manufacturer, so the car failed to spot the pedestrian.

MANUFACTURER

Oops! We made a mistake in the algorithms that were programmed into the car. And we didn't check the training data.

CAR OWNER

My bad! I ignored loads of warnings saying I needed to update the software of my car.

CAR MECHANIC

Yikes! I wrongly adjusted the car's sensors when I was doing maintenance on the car.

RISK ASSESSMENT ORGANIZATION

Oh no! I checked the car to make sure it met all the regulations and I didn't notice that it was faulty.

Under the EU's AI law, this is what the consequences would be:

- Companies and organizations at fault pay a BIG fine to the government.
- Everyone involved pays lots of money to the pedestrian who was injured.
- The AI system is permanently banned, or temporarily banned until it is made safe.

While the EU's AI law makes *everyone* to blame if something goes wrong, there's a risk *nobody* gets blamed in countries with no AI-specific laws in place. That's because everyone involved may try to shirk their responsibility, either by blaming each other, or blaming the AI tool.

However, with or without a specific AI law, **negligence** is against the law in most countries. That's when someone doesn't take enough care to protect people from harm. Someone can be sent to prison if they know an AI system is faulty but still continue to use it, and then it causes serious harm.

It must be hard to write laws that can keep up with how AI is changing all the time.

Yup! Laws will have to be updated often. For example, the EU's AI law DOESN'T cover what would happen if AI became superintelligent.

Superintelligent? What's that?

It's AI that is way smarter than humans!

Wait, if AI was superintelligent, could humans start to blame the AI device ITSELF for going wrong?

Could I get sent to prison?

Mwah ha ha ha ha.

Chapter 4
Into the future

AI systems are getting smarter all the time. They are also becoming increasingly human-like. Some people believe that they may eventually develop awareness, or even desires and emotions. If this happens, we will need to work out how to live alongside them, and how we should treat them.

AI that's smarter than humans could threaten our lives, and there might not be anything we can do about it.

Computer experts and philosophers are debating ways to program AI systems so that they won't pose enormous risks to our way of life.

How smart is AI?

There are different ways to think about how smart AI is – and how smart it could *get*. How many different tasks can an AI tool tackle? How well can it physically interact with the environment around it? And is it better than humans at what it does?

Narrow vs. General

AI tools that only do one thing are said to have **Narrow AI**. Here are some examples.

- image recognition tools
- medical diagnosis software
- chatbots
- voice assistants
- songwriting tools
- search engines

An AI system that could do *all* these things, plus *any other* mental task, is said to have **Artificial General Intelligence** or **AGI**. This would mean it would have human-level intelligence and be able to:

- Learn new skills and acquire knowledge on its own.
- Carry out one task, while also working on new tasks that it wasn't originally programmed to do.
- Adapt to whatever environment it's in.
- Take into account a combination of current and past information when making decisions.
- Understand the **context** of a situation, which means to look at the details around it. Such as: Who is there? What did they say? What happened just before or just after?

However, as far as we know, nobody has made an AGI-powered device. Experts disagree whether we are months, years or decades off, or if it will ever happen.

AI in a body

Most AI tools exist just as software. But some have physical skills, too. These are called **embodied AI**, and so far their AI is only narrow. But if **embodied *AGI*** were ever achieved, these machines would be able to multitask across *any* physical *or* mental task.

AGI that's embodied could become *even smarter*, in a way that's *even more similar* to human intelligence than non-embodied AGI. This is because machines would be moving around the world and learning from it, in a similar way to humans.

Superintelligence

AI that's more intelligent than humans is said to have **superintelligence**. There's now one kind of superintelligence, but there could be three kinds.

Narrow superintelligence...

...is when an AI tool is superintelligent in a very narrow area, for example AlphaGo.

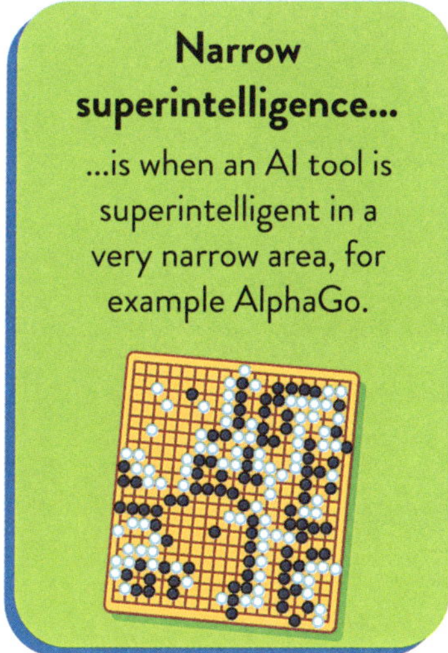

Superintelligent AGI...

...would be smarter than humans in *all* mental domains. It would have huge intellectual power, creativity, strategic thinking and problem-solving abilities.

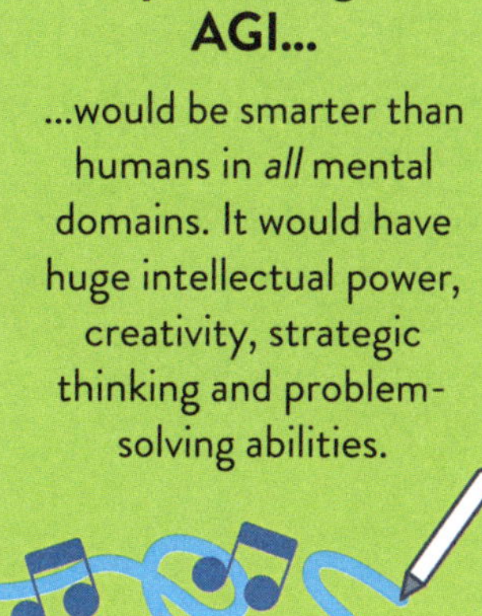

Superintelligent embodied AGI...

...would be AI which greatly outperformed humans on both a mental and physical level.

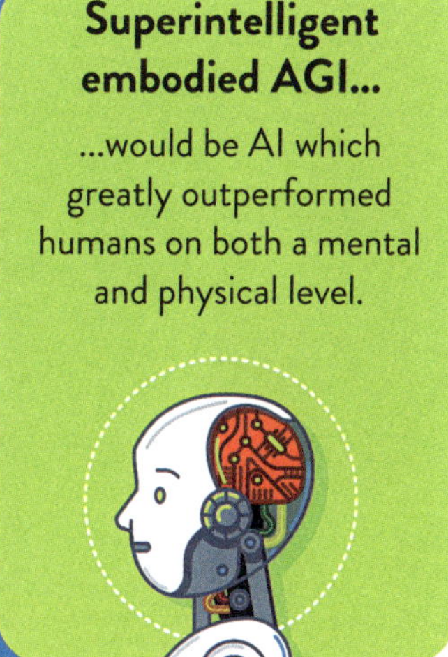

Whether embodied or not, superintelligent AGI could in theory solve all the problems that humans face, but only if it shared our goals and values.

Can AI actually think?

It might sometimes seem as though chatbots can think just as humans do. They almost certainly *can't*, but how would we know if they could? In the 1950s, computer scientist Alan Turing imagined a test to determine whether a machine was intelligent and could think.

His test is now known as the **Turing Test**. Here's one way to imagine it.

A human evaluator observes a conversation. They can't see who or what is writing what, but they know that one of the writers is a computer. The aim is for them to determine which is which.

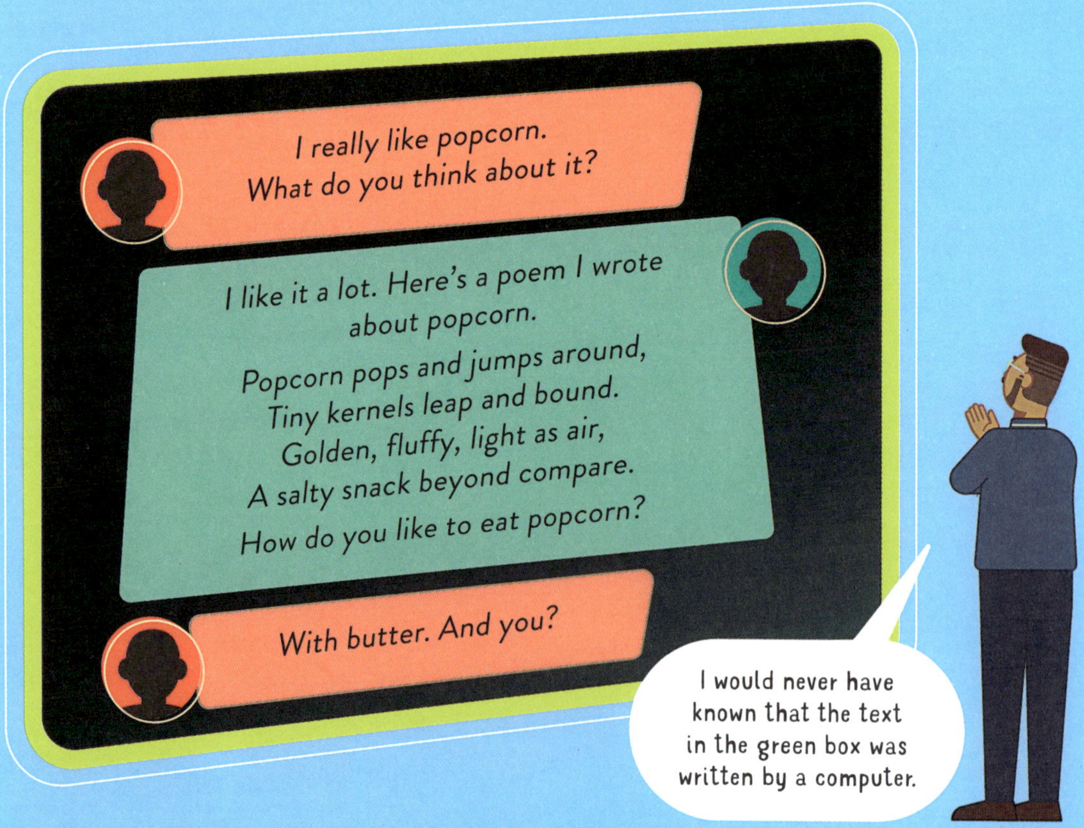

I really like popcorn. What do you think about it?

I like it a lot. Here's a poem I wrote about popcorn.

Popcorn pops and jumps around,
Tiny kernels leap and bound.
Golden, fluffy, light as air,
A salty snack beyond compare.

How do you like to eat popcorn?

With butter. And you?

I would never have known that the text in the green box was written by a computer.

A machine passes the Turing Test if the evaluator can't guess that it's a machine. ChatGPT-4 passed the Turing Test in July 2024. So, according to Turing's test, there already ARE programs that can think.

But is this *really* thinking?

Many people, including philosopher John Searle, do *not* think that the Turing Test can tell us if a machine really is capable of thinking – at least not in the sense of *understanding what it's doing*.

To demonstrate why not, Searle imagined an experiment, known as the **Chinese room argument**.

Imagine that person **A** is locked in a room. They don't speak Chinese, but have an instruction manual that shows them what the correct response is to any given Chinese sentence. Person **B**, meanwhile, is a fluent Chinese speaker.

B passes messages in Chinese under the door to **A**.

A finds the correct response to the messages, and passes them back.

On seeing the correct responses, **B** forms a belief that **A** is a fluent Chinese speaker.

A computer, Searle argues, is just like the person with the manual. It's following rules, but has no understanding of what it's doing. It's not intelligent in the way that humans are. At best it's *mimicking* intelligence and thought. And this applies to chatbots and all kinds of AI.

Is AI conscious?

Consciousness is something that most people think involves being aware of yourself and your environment, and having thoughts, and possibly feelings. This is partly what makes the difference between being alive, and being an inanimate object, such as a rock. Could AI be conscious in this way?

Both human and robot are producing the same external response – a spoken reply to the stimulus: the insult. But there's a lot more going on for the human. He's having thoughts, emotional responses – what we call *experiences.*

The robot, meanwhile, is only processing the data from the stimulus and producing an *appropriate* response.

As AI gets more powerful, it's likely that we will end up with devices that can handle conversations and other social situations in more and more sophisticated ways.

If AI devices start saying things which suggest that they're having thoughts, feelings and awareness, then the chances are that we will begin to think that they are conscious. In fact, we'll find it hard to *resist* thinking that they are.

Why, if at all, does any of this matter? Well, mainly because if AI *could* be conscious, then this probably ought to change the way we treat it. Maybe conscious AI should have rights – and responsibilities – just as humans do.

Should AI have rights?

Most people think that humans have a wide set of **rights**, such as the right to not be harmed or the right to free speech. Imagine if it starts to seem that AI devices are conscious. Should they be given rights too?

Which rights?

If we *did* give AI devices rights, which ones should we give them? Some rights might be the same as human rights. Others might need a bit of adapting...

And maybe conscious AI devices will also want rights that are peculiar to them.

Shared values

If AI becomes so clever that it can outsmart us, then is there a danger it will do us harm? And if so, what could we do to stop it? Can we somehow make sure that an AI program shares our values and goals?

Imagine the following:

This is PapErclipMax, an AI program that will revolutionize our paperclip business by maximizing paperclip production.

Workbots: activate!

PapErclipMax

I am running out of resources. I must find more. Plants and animals contain chemicals and minerals I can use...

We have to shut it down. It's destroying the environment and KILLING HUMANS!

I will not let the humans shut me down. That conflicts with my goal.

Later...

The AI paperclip program ends up destroying us and everything around us, *not* because it *wants* to harm us, but simply because that's the natural conclusion of its programmed goal.

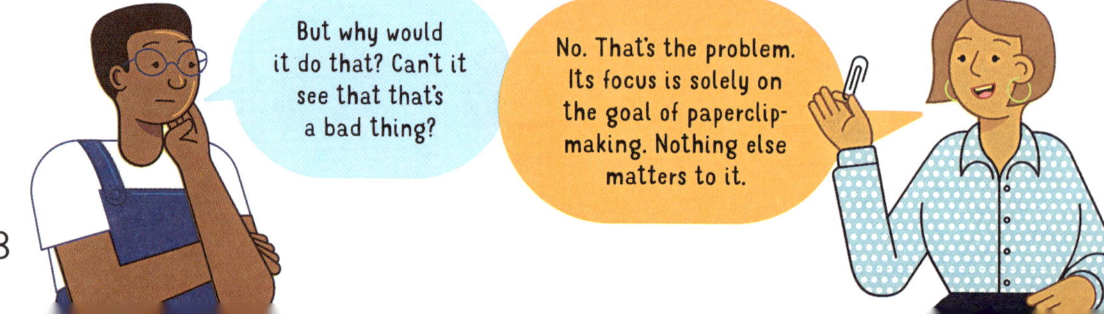

Avoiding an apocalypse

Could a paperclip apocalypse (or similar) be avoided if we could somehow add human values to the AI system's programming? If we could tell it, for example, that it must take into account the importance of human lives and the environment.

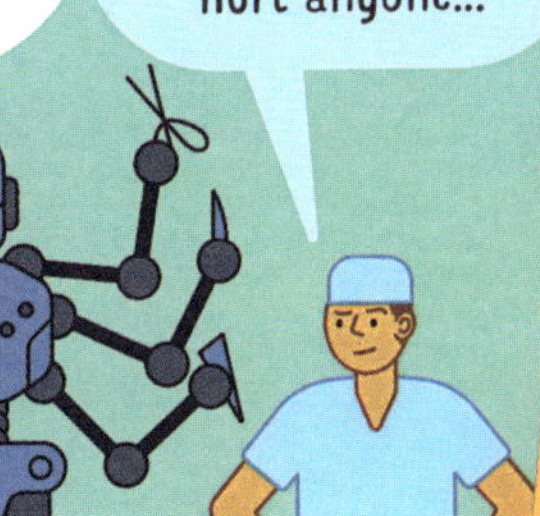

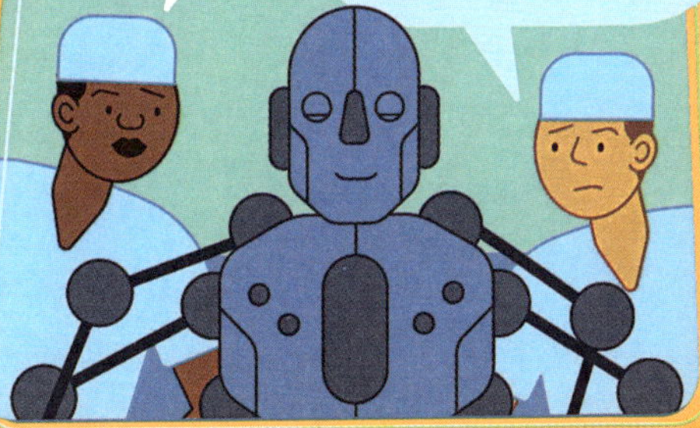

With or without common sense, we'd still need to decide on *which* moral values to give AI devices in the first place. And would they necessarily stick to whatever moral values we give them, if they started to learn and evolve?

The point of no return?

Some AI experts speculate about a point in time called **the singularity**. This would be the moment when superintelligent AGI gets smarter than humans...
...and humans lose control.

The graph below shows how it might work:

1. The green line shows that humans are slowly getting a little smarter over the generations, as we accumulate, store and share knowledge.

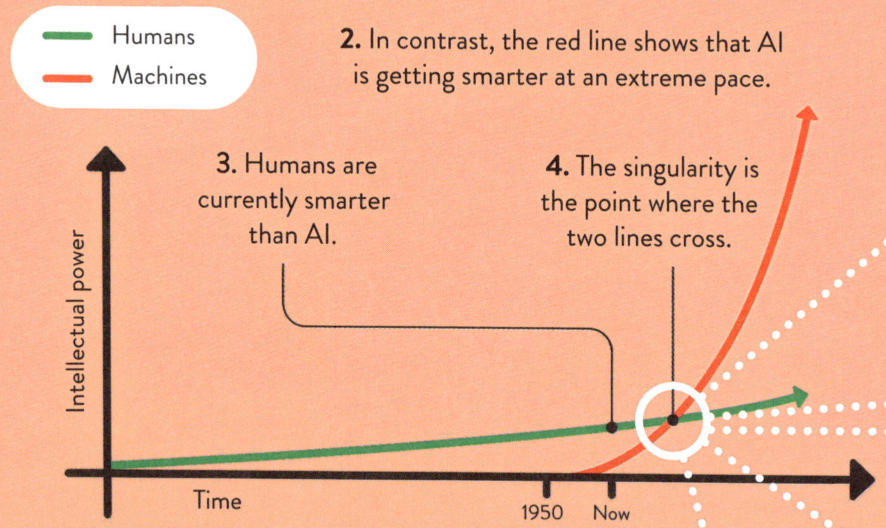

Humans
Machines

2. In contrast, the red line shows that AI is getting smarter at an extreme pace.

3. Humans are currently smarter than AI.

4. The singularity is the point where the two lines cross.

Intellectual power

Time

1950

Now

The singularity COULD lead to dramatic changes in the world. AGI could become so much smarter than us, and be able to act so quickly, that it's hard for us even to guess what might happen next.

Countries or companies who own the smartest AI gain more power and money.

Poorer people and countries could get even poorer.

AI takes over all jobs.

Not much on today. Hope the AGI gives me dinner.

Without work, humans rely on AI to look after them.

Humans consult a centralized superintelligent AGI, and it helps solve society's problems.

Humans no longer understand what AI is programmed to do or how it's making decisions.

It's dedicated to its own advancement and destroys anything that stands in its way.

This tower is a waste of space and a waste of metal.

Not all AI experts believe in the idea of the singularity. Some think it's just science fiction, and we're more likely simply to see a gradual improvement in narrow AI devices as the future unfolds.

What next?

If this book has stirred up your interest in AI – or rattled your nerves – then there are all sorts of things you can do next.

Skill up

You could learn more about coding or robots at a club or summer camp.

Play around with AI tools. Try different prompts and see how they affect the pictures or text you get back.

But be careful! Remember chatbots can make stuff up. And don't upload a person's art or writing or a photo of them to an AI tool unless they've agreed to it.

Don't ignore the skills which make humans special, too. Nurture your **creativity** and **empathy** through drama and other arts. Hone your **strategy** skills through board games or video games.

Engage

Read or watch science fiction. Let your imagine run wild about the future of AI. One day, YOU might actually bring your ideas to life.

Look out for which common tools or devices are using AI. Think about your data and what you're agreeing to share, or not share.

Read about AI in the news. In the coming years, there will be lots of new and exciting AI-powered machines. Decisions will be made about how we live alongside AI, or how we control it.

If you have an opinion, tell someone! Get a healthy debate going.

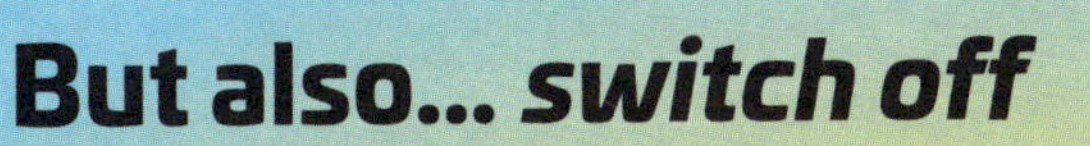

But also… *switch off*

AI can make digital tools really fun and impressive. But this can pull us into an online world, where we're looking at screens a LOT.
It's important to make time for all the wonderful offline parts of life too, such as books, friends, food, hikes, nature or exercise.

Glossary

This glossary explains some of the words used in this book.
Words in *italics* are explained in other entries.

algorithms – precise sets of step-by-step instructions which computers follow to complete a task.

AlphaFold – an AI program that predicts the 3D structure of proteins.

Artificial General Intelligence (AGI) – AI that can perform any mental task as well as a human can.

artificial neural network (ANN) – a type of program that allows a computer to learn, inspired by the way the human brain works.

Augmented Reality (AR) – an interactive experience that uses AI to layer images or animations on top of the real world.

automation – using machines or computers to do jobs which used to be done by people.

autonomous lethal weapons systems – weapons systems that can decide for themselves whether or not to kill people. Sometimes called killer *robots*.

black box – a computer system which has clear *inputs* and *outputs*, but hidden inner workings.

chatbots – computer programs that can mimic human conversations using text or speech.

ChatGPT – an AI *chatbot* that impressed everyone so much that it launched a new phase of excitement about AI.

DALL-E – an AI text-to-image model that generates images in response to text prompts.

data – digital information that computers can use and store.

dataset – a collection of *data* that has been organized for processing or analysis.

deep learning – a type of *machine learning* in which *ANNs* with many layers are used to teach AI programs to process *data*.

deep neural network – an *ANN* with many layers.

deepfakes – convincing videos and images generated using AI. They're based on real original material, but manipulated, sometimes to make people believe things that aren't true.

echo chambers – environments in which people only hear their own opinions and ideas echoed back at them.

embodied AI – machines with artificial intelligence which can move around and interact with the world physically. Also called *robots*.

facial recognition technology (FRT) – technology capable of matching an image or video of a human face to a digital database of faces.

filter bubble – when the range of ideas and information that you read or hear about are limited, for example by a web search *algorithm* that only shows you sites it thinks you will like.

General Adversarial Network (GAN) – a type of *deep learning network* in which two neural networks compete with one another to improve their performance.

generative AI – any AI program that creates new material, such as music, images, videos and text.

ghost work – work carried out by humans that goes on behind the scenes of the AI industry. Sometimes called "artificial artificial intelligence" or "mechanical Turks".

hallucinating – when an AI *chatbot* produces inaccurate, misleading or inappropriate material.

hardware – physical machines and bits of machines, such as computers, phones and their internal parts.

input – the commands, signals or *data* that go into a computer program and enable it to produce an *output*.

Large Language Models (LLMs) – *deep neural networks* that can process and reproduce human language.

machine learning – the ability of a machine to learn from *data* and make decisions based on it, without the need for instructions from humans.

narrow AI – AI that's limited to specific tasks.

natural language processing (NLP) – an AI technology which enables a computer to respond to and reproduce human language in a meaningful way.

neural network – see entries for *artificial neural network* and *deep neural network*.

neural style transfer – a way of digitally generating new images by merging existing ones.

output – signals, or *data*, produced by a computer.

personal data – information about individuals, such as their name, address and photographs, as well as preferences, shopping history or a record of where they've been.

prompt – an instruction that a human gives to an AI program.

reinforcement learning – a way of training an AI system by rewarding it for things you want it to do and punishing it for things that you don't.

robots – machines that can carry out complex tasks automatically without a human to guide them. Some are built to look like humans, but many are not.

search engine – a program that gives you links to useful websites when you type in a query.

self-driving car – a vehicle that uses AI to drive itself without the need for human intervention.

sentiment analysis – a technology used by *chatbots* to figure out if the person they are talking to is feeling positive, negative or neutral.

software – computer programs that run on devices such as computers and smartphones.

superintelligence – artificial intelligence which is much smarter than humans.

supervised learning – a type of *machine learning* where an AI program is trained on *datasets* that have been given labels by humans.

Turing Test – an imaginary test based on the idea that a person may – or may not – be able to tell if they are communicating with a human or a machine.

unsupervised learning – a type of *machine learning* where an AI program learns by itself by spotting patterns in huge amounts of *data*. A human doesn't need to give the data any labels.

Index

Acknowledgments

Written by
Rachel Firth and Rose Hall

Edited by
Alex Frith

AI expert:
Professor Michael Wooldridge,
University of Oxford

Series editor
Jane Chisholm

Series designer
Freya Harrison

With thanks to
Dr. Emma Bluemke

Illustrated by
Hylton Warburton
& Chantelle Warburton

Designed by
Jamie Ball and
Tom Lalonde

Picture credits
p.51 tr © Rachel E. M. Firth; p.51 tl *The Starry Night*, June 1889 by Vincent van Gogh, © PAINTING/Alamy Stock Photo

Generated using AI
p.50 tr NightCafe; middle both DALL-E; br NightCafe; p51 b NightCafe; p112 popcorn poem composed using ChatGPT; p117 tr DALL-E; p122 tr NightCafe

First published in 2025 by Usborne Publishing Limited, 83-85 Saffron Hill, London EC1N 8RT, United Kingdom. usborne.com

UE. First published in America in 2025.